ANCIENT WISDOM for MODERN IGNORANCE

ANCIENT WISDOM for MODERN IGNORANCE

SWAMI B.V. TRIPURARI

CLARION CALL PUBLISHING
EUGENE, OREGON • ROME, ITALY • VRINDAVANA, INDIA

For more information about the Gaudiya Vaishnava Society, please correspond with the secretary at:

Sri Sri Gaura-Nityananda Audarya Ashrama
325 River Road
Eugene, OR 97404
USA
(503) 461-5760

Other centers:
Rūpānuga Bhajana Āśrama
177 Rangaji Ka Nagla
Vṛndāvana, U.P. 281121
India

Śrī Kṛṣṇa Chaitanya Āśramam
Pandimuttam, P.O.
Thiruvanthapuram
Kerala 645027
India

COPYEDITOR:
Vṛndāranya devī dāsī

DESIGNER:
Paurnamasi devī dāsī

COMPUTER ASSISTANCE
WITH THE COVER:
Kayrin Gregory

Library of Congress
Catalog Card Number: 94-68580
ISBN 1-886069-11-5

© Clarion Call Publishing 1994.
All rights reserved. Printed in the
United States of America.

DEDICATION

TO MY

spiritual master,

His Divine Grace

A. C. Bhaktivedanta

Swami Prabhupāda,

and all of

his followers.

TABLE OF CONTENTS

Introduction .... page *ix*

CULTURAL CONQUEST

Social Paradigm .... page 3
Spirit Of The Environment .... page 13
Who Discovered America? .... page 27
Sacred Cow .... page 39
Raga And All That Jazz .... page 49

KNOWLEDGE OVER NESCIENCE?

The Case For Continence .... page 65
Life In The Womb .... page 77
Making Sense With Scents .... page 85
Ayurveda or Allopathy? .... page 93

VOICE OF TRANSCENDENCE

The Heart Of Compassion .... page 107
Demystifying Mystic Powers .... page 117
Old Age Common Sense For
    New Age Nonsense .... page 127
Hallowed Be Thy Name .... page 137
Ecstasy—Can We Live Without It? .... page 147

About the Author .... page 159
References .... page 161
Index .... page 163

INTRODUCTION

IT IS WISE TO LOOK BACK before looking ahead, for the past often repeats itself. Yet all too often we do not look back; we do not learn from our mistakes. Nor do we learn from those wise persons who have been right all along. Ignorance can be very stubborn. Yet wisdom is very persistent, much of it spoken in centuries past continues to speak to us today.

The essays in this book were written with a view to address the quality of our life. They draw heavily on India's ancient spiritual heritage of theistic Vedanta, interfacing India's spiritual and cultural wisdom and devotional heart with our times. This interface should prove useful for those who are already discouraged with the direction humanity is heading as well as for those who still hold fast to ideas that have seen better days. For those now disenchanted with industrialization and scientific materialism as well as pseudospirituality, India's ancient spiritual heritage provides a rich alternative. Those who continue to subscribe to materialistic dogma, having written off the spiritual out of frustration, will find in these articles a formidable challenge to their worldview. It is a challenge well-reasoned, much unlike that which is offered by the materially compromised spiritual West.

India has had considerable impact on the West over the last thirty years, ancient India that is. Modern India is a westernized India that has either lost sight of its ancient culture or believes in its spiritual heritage without understanding much more of it than the surface. Indologist A. L. Basham tells us of the noble past of Mother India in his seminal work, *The Wonder That Was India*.

ANCIENT WISDOM

But where is India today? It can be seen in mainstream America from time to time in jest, where truth is often found. Stars and starlets joke of future and past lives, and TV hosts have been known to attribute their successes and failures to the "laugh" rather than "law" of karma. More importantly, it can be found in the hopes and hearts of many Westerners seeking an alternative to their own modern materialistic culture.

Gita Mehta, famous New York author and socialite, has commented on America's interest in India; however, she has acknowledged only the mainstream flirtation of the American public with India's spiritual heritage. Her book *Karma Cola* depicts Westerners superficially exploring an India, Vedic India, which Mehta believes in but says no one is following, including herself. Why not? one might ask, if she believes in it. Unfortunately, she represents the westernized Indian who has lost sight of her spiritual heritage.

Yet that is difficult to do, as her continued "belief" attests, for India, spiritual India, is indeed a wonder, one that indologists like Basham would be glad to know lives on. Mainstream America may like to laugh at India and those interested in her rich spiritual culture, and Indians like Mehta may be content to be affluent Uncle Toms, but many people from the western world have become charmed by spiritual India, its practical and esoteric insights. They have chosen India's ancient wisdom over our modern ignorance.

In our diet, music, health care, science, sexuality, and religion the influence of ancient spiritual India can be traced out. Subtle this influence may be, but after all, that is also India, subtle and sublime.

Vegetarianism is on the rise, even popular. McDonald's has brought out everything from fish and salad to now in some European countries a veggie burger. McDonald's is under siege by Jeremy Rifkin, scientific heretic turned en-

INTRODUCTION

ronmentalist and author of best-seller *Beyond Beef*. Rifkin, influenced deeply by spiritual India, has organized protests at McDonalds' throughout the United States, clamoring for a veggie burger. Naturopathic health care has risen dramatically. *USA Today* reported that an alarmingly large percentage of Americans preferred, at least in theory, naturopathy to allopathy, and ancient India's *ayurveda*, which is on the rise in America, represents the oldest, most comprehensive naturopathic health care system on earth.

Several years ago Christian fundamentalists identified "new age philosophy" as their greatest enemy since the fall of communism. They further identified generic Indian philosophical themes, such as karma, vegetarianism, and reincarnation, underlying much of new age thought. One out of every three Catholics in the United States believes in reincarnation, heresy that it is.

Perhaps the most significant example of India's spiritual influence on the industrialized world is found in the realm of science. For the longest time consciousness was not something to discuss in a laboratory. Objective science, however, while penetrating the atomic particle, found, much to their surprise, that the observer influences the experiment. Now with the entrance of subjective reality, scientists have to talk about consciousness on the scientific stage. And those who have the integrity to admit that consciousness must be discussed, Nobel laureates included, have turned to India, the *Upanishads*, and the *Bhagavad-gītā*, where consciousness has been discussed for thousands of years. Books abound, best-sellers, which interface eastern mysticism with modern science. Ancient India's spiritual wisdom has made inroads into the priesthood of the faith of modern science. It has captured the minds and hearts of critical thinkers of the West and has created hope that life is more than atomic particles bouncing randomly. The world is not on the verge of wholesale change, but it is changing gradually in the direction of some of the noblest thoughts of our planet's ancient cultures, of which Indian culture is arguably older and wiser than all.

We want to be happy; we want to love. We are starving for feeling, a feeling that merely "having" does not fulfill. Eastern philosophy, and the devotional heart of India's Vedanta in particular, can fill the empty shopping bag of our Western accomplishments. And when it has done so, we will not feel that we have been conquered, rather we will feel liberated from the oppression that the prevailing yet faltering scientific industrial paradigm fosters.

While the West has been bent on changing the East, this conversion is one that takes place on the surface. Good packaging is something we are good at, but delivering the goods of a qualitatively better life is where we have fallen short. The dog is running on four legs and barking. Modern humanity is riding on four wheels and blowing its horn. Is there any categorical difference between these two?

Something, however, in all of this must be said for the Western seeker, who is bringing to life concepts from the East, while many from the East remain asleep to their own spiritual heritage. They are noble people who are prepared to look beyond their own cultural setting for a solution to universal problems. That the answers should lie largely in a distant land is not surprising any more than the wonder that a "foreigner" is discovering them and disseminating them. The truth transcends East and West while revealing itself through these mediums. We are not to argue with this, for revelation is the truth's prerogative. We are but instruments of divine will.

CULTURAL CONQUEST

AN INDIAN SAGE
WAS ONCE ASKED WHAT
HE THOUGHT OF
WESTERN CIVILIZATION.
HE REPLIED,
"I THINK IT IS A GOOD IDEA.
WHEN WILL IT BEGIN?"

SOCIAL PARADIGM

I REMEMBER MY SEVENTH GRADE teacher telling me about India's horrific caste system. She taught that India's caste system was the height of social injustice. Yet somehow I could not agree with her, although at the time I did not have a logical response to the contrary.

All that India meant to me was the tall, slender Indian lady draped in a silken sari with bangles on her arms, a ring in her nose, and a red dot on her forehead, who I would see from time to time with her young son, walking through the corridor at lunch hour.

She would bring a special lunch for her son, and to me she represented something mysterious that was somehow deeper and richer than all the "facts" I was gathering in school. It was hard for me to believe that the great social evil, the caste system, as described in my seventh grade world history class, was an accurate portrayal of the culture of India. Later I came to find that my skepticism was warranted.

Progressive, socially conscious zealots, especially in the land of "rights"—Hometown, USA—are quick to point out social inequalities, both at home and abroad. Today the outcry for human rights is one that is hard for even the world's most oppressive regimes to ignore. Following the Reagan administration, conservative President Bush won the election by condemning liberalism, calling it the "L" word; ironically, however, historian Albert Schlesinger recently pointed out that Bush's call for a "kinder and more gentle nation" exemplified those in power yielding to the rising force of liberalism.

ANCIENT WISDOM

Liberalism that leads to kinder and more gentle nations is certainly desirable. If this kind of liberalism is on the rise, it is encouraging, because it indicates progress in the spiritual direction. We want equality for all, and, after all, we have heard that "all men (and women) are created equal." So a social system that determines a person's social status and rights by the family in which he or she is born would seem—to be generous—outdated. And India's caste system appears to do just that. Four orders of occupation are outlined: the intellectual, the martial, the mercantile, and the laboring class, and in whichever family one is born in, the dye is cast, and one's life's status is fixed. It is thought that one's social status can change only by achieving a higher birth in the next life. This social system seems contradictory to the spiritual values of ancient India, which hearken us to see the equality of all living beings. How could a spiritual culture have a repressive social system?

Obviously, it can't. In reality, the repressive caste system is not representative of spiritual India, but of modern India. India's spirituality does not foster the caste system, but it does, however, recognize a natural fourfold social structure. The division of society determined by birthright (the caste system) is but a vitiated form of another social system that recognizes a social structure that undeniably exists not only in India but throughout the entire world.

This social structure is called *varnashrama*. The Sanskrit word *varna* literally means "color," but it refers to the "color" of the mind, or one's temperament, and not to the body. It therefore implies a standard of conduct or mode of occupation that naturally corresponds with one's mental disposition or karmic tendency. The *varnashrama* social system divides human effort into four classes of occupation by determining one's karmic leaning, not by what family one takes birth in. It first takes into consideration one's spiritual status and then determines one's material propensity.

In India today the outer structure of the *varnashrama* system is acknowledged, but the spiritual substance behind it is severely lacking. Because of this, India's social system may appear at a glance more dehumanizing than both capitalism and communism, but history reveals that both of these modern forms of government are corruptions of the *varnashrama* institution.

How strict observance of one's birth lines came to determine one's status in India is somewhat understandable inasmuch as birth in a particular family dictates considerably how we will think. Especially in a society where the family unit is strong, children tend to be molded in accordance with their parent's views: sons often take up the family business, for example. Moreover, following a spiritual worldview, souls tend to be born into material families whose values mirror their stage of spiritual evolution. All of this is relative, however, and there are many exceptions. Sometimes children seem to have been born into the wrong family in that they differ so much from the interests of their parents. Almost every family has a "black sheep," not in the sense of an evil son or daughter, but a child who does not identify with the family's values. Thus, India's overemphasis on the importance of birth rather than on each individual's qualities and inner attitude has corrupted her social system.

To appreciate how both the communist and capitalist ideologies are but the *varnashrama* system in decay, a more detailed explanation of what the *varnashrama* system is and how it works will be helpful. As we will see, *varnashrama* is sometimes manifest and sometimes not, but its influence nonetheless continues to exist throughout all societies.

ANCIENT WISDOM

Manifest *varnashrama* consists of recognizing material inequalities and taking advantage of them to derive our inherent spiritual equality. Unlike materially-based social systems, *varnashrama* does not artificially attempt to find equality through material adjustment. Rather, it finds beauty and higher truth in our material inequality. Because in this system success is not determined by material advancement, material inequality is not indicative of one person being inferior to another, any more than an apple is inferior to a banana. Both are valuable in their own right. Unlike the modern democratic ideology, which attempts to reduce everyone to the same set of basically material values, equating happiness with material advancement, *varnashrama* recognizes the uniqueness of all people and directs them toward spiritual values.

The *varnashrama* system views all living beings as spiritual entities within material bodies, and progress in this system is spiritual development that leads in the direction of transcending birth, death, and all material inequality. Ultimately, *varnashrama* culminates in the development of love of Godhead. Since the soul or consciousness is the very basis for experience, it is most practical to have a social arrangement that is designed to foster experience of the soul, by which all other material experience can be accurately understood. We may observe that material, goal-oriented social systems do just the opposite: they either obscure the soul altogether or leave room for the half-baked conception of a soul composed of both spirit and matter.

The division of labor (*varna*) and station of direct spiritual culture (*ashrama*) in the *varnashrama* social body can be compared to the division of our bodies: head, arms, torso, and legs. The intellectual class is the head of society. Although smaller than any other class, its detached influence permeates the entire society. The intellectual class writes the books of the society and conducts research for the advancement of knowledge. The arms of society are the martial class. Those who belong to the martial class engage in "hands-on" management; they are the government administrators and valorous leaders who organize while taking advice from the intellectual class. They too are highly intellectual but possess a passion for administration. The mercantile class, synonymous with the agriculturists, is the torso of society and is profit-oriented. The laboring class, as the legs of society, assists others and provides necessary forms of relaxation, such as arts and entertainment.

All societies are made up of people with these dispositions. By examining the basic values of any society, we can also find four basic domains: knowledge, status, wealth, and pleasure. All human effort is aimed at these values. Thus these values also create the four *varnas*. For example, if wealth-seeking is our goal, we will be confined within the commercial perspective and experience everything in light of profiteering. The ancient Vedic culture, in which *varnashrama* was fully operational, recognized these different mentalities to be manifestations of material nature's karmic influence. These influences, or modes of material nature, were perceived to pervade every aspect of material life.

The forces of creation, maintenance, and destruction, which are operative in all spheres of life governed by time and space, are considered to constitute our mental makeup. Our goals and values are determined by that makeup, and regardless of any other external conditions, that innate karmic disposition will determine our working propensity. When we are engaged in accordance with our karmic tendency, we can be productive, and when the governing worldview does not cause us to feel that we are in any way inferior to another, regardless of our material social status (by way of promoting spiritual development), we can be peaceful.

To safeguard against corruption and exploitation, the institution of *ashrama* is essential. This side of *varnashrama* is especially important for the intellectual and administrative classes because they lead the society. Society's leaders and intellectuals must pass through all four stations of spiritual culture. This begins with student life (*brahmacharya*), in which celibacy is mandatory, as is austerity and the practice of meditation under the guidance of a spiritual mentor. For most, this is followed by married life (*grihashta*) until the children are prepared to raise families of their own. Married life is the time for "worldliness" tempered by one's earlier education in spiritual values and one's meditative experience. After married life, men and women enter into retired life (*vanaprashta*) and prepare themselves ultimately for a life of renunciation (*sannyasa*), in which they free themselves from all attachment to that which is temporary. In this way, *ashrama* helps insure that the leaders of society are free from false possessiveness and the tendency to exploit others.

When the most influential sections of society advocate spiritual values and exemplify a high standard of spiritual pursuit, all sections of society experience a unity in diversity. While all people are variously engaged in accordance with their diverse material natures, and thus form subcultures within the larger culture, they are unified in spiritual pursuit. *Varnashrama* synthesizes material difference with spiritual oneness, making God the center of society and offering the fruits of labor unto Godhead. All labor, although different, is seen as one—devotion.

Far from being a primitive or foreign social structure, *varnashrama* is a highly sophisticated arrangement for harmonious living, both materially and spiritually, which in-

SOCIAL PARADIGM

volves organizing society from a spiritual perspective. Western governments have emphasized the separation of spiritual pursuit and the affairs of the state in the name of protecting spiritual liberty; but, in effect, they have made our spiritual interest a secondary concern. If we want to "believe," we can, but the state is not about to investigate the nature of reality enough to understand the spiritual nature of consciousness and organize society based on such findings. By contrast, the *varnashrama* system organizes society's material efforts in such a way that all of its members can experience the real self.

Varnashrama's external classification of people may remind us of what we learned about medieval Europe's feudal system, as does the idea of any God-centered society. Indeed the similarities between these two social systems strongly suggests ties between Europe and India. The feudal system could very well be seen as Europe's version of *varnashrama,* while the breakdown of the feudal system has given rise to our present-day Western social systems. Although our modern social systems are usually viewed as improvements from feudal times, they may also be viewed along with the feudal system as the breakdown of *varnashrama.*

Medieval Europe's corrupt form of government with its "divine kings," "holy wars," and exploitation of the masses, causes us to shy away from the idea of a spiritual God-centered form of government. Even today, religious fundamentalists stand out as beacons of totalitarianism, threatening our freedom of thought. We must remember that mere belief in religious dogma is far from self-realization. Full-fledged *varnashrama* does not advocate fanatical religious belief but actual transcendental experience and God consciousness for which there are objective symptoms. *Varnashrama's* successful implementation depends on experience of the spiritual self, an experience that can be accessed through genuine traditions.

The Protestant Reformation of 1529 C.E. was a reactionary movement that overthrew the spiritually corrupt feudal system with its four classes of pontiffs, overlords, vassals, and serfs. The feudal system was only a primitive approximation of actual *varnashrama:* when its intellectual priestly class became polluted with worldly ambition, their power—a moral and spiritual force—was lost. In this condition their preeminence appeared no longer justifiable in the eyes of the administrative martial class of kings. When the administrators sever themselves from spiritual guidance, they become tyrants who only mouth religious dogma, using it to justify anything and everything. What follows, as history has shown, is such a mercantile/agriculturist uprising as the French Revolution (1789 C.E.). People who are money-minded and clever in business build industry and trade, and in their unquenchable thirst for wealth, they exploit the laboring class, which in turn leads to further revolt, the likes of which was seen in the Russian Revolution of 1917 C.E.

Thus *varnashrama* is quite relevant to us today. As the concept of *varnashrama* moved west from ancient India to medieval Europe, it became polluted. From that corrupted form of *varnashrama,* our present sociopolitical systems have appeared. What we are now experiencing is the decline of *varnashrama.* Both capitalism, the mercantile government, and communism, the government of the laboring class, are forms of government in which wealth and material fulfillment are the predominant values. Communism is openly atheistic, and thus in pursuit of material values. Although God is allowed in the capitalist society, capitalists pray to God for the same material wealth that the atheists find without acknowledging God. *Varnashrama,* on the other hand, is led by unswerving righteousness

SOCIAL PARADIGM

and genuine spiritual understanding. Today's social systems consist of merely varying degrees of decay in manifest *varnashrama*—although all of the four classes continue to exist, their status is either not admitted or not properly implemented.

If we objectively view the present-day struggle between the political left and right as a decay of the superior social system of ancient India, we can conclude that the modern ideologies of capitalism and communism do not have the potential to create a truly just and merciful society. The problem that we are faced with in advocating the superiority of the *varnashrama* system is that those in power are not about to move aside. Nonetheless, the rising interest in genuine spiritual experience cannot be denied or legislated away; it is a subtle yet powerful force, and in time it will prevail.

The West's reemerging interest in the transcendent is a natural and ultimately unavoidable development. We have almost reached the bottom of social decay in the forms of the exploitation known as capitalism, which thrives on greed; and communism, which inevitably leads to brutality. From here there is only one way to go—up. In his insightful article "Blueprint for Social Harmony," printed in *Sri Mayapur* magazine, Dr. William Deadwyler has summed up the hopelessness of our world's two most prominent social systems: "Both are rooted in the past and are expressions of social putrefaction. Certainly, European and American society in the twentieth century has become fatally infected by *vaishya* [mercantile] values run amok. But *shudra* [labor] values run amok are no improvement. As a totally materialistic philosophy, communism fosters rather than eliminates the seeds of exploitation and conflict, encouraging the very conditions it seeks to ameliorate. Consequently, under communism there will never be a society

ANCIENT WISDOM

free from the domination of one group by another, of the many by the few, and that domination will be carried on by the most brutal means possible. Both capitalist and communist ideologies are products of exploitation and envy, and neither therefore can hope to eliminate them. They cannot offer release from the process of social degeneration because they are created by it."

The upliftment of human society rests in the hands of those yearning for and those already experiencing what is most natural—the spiritual dimension. A new society must have at its head a class of people who are free from material attachment and can actually do good for others, being free themselves from the very causes of human suffering: lust, avarice, envy, and the like. A truly intelligent ruling class sees intelligence as subordinate to the soul and sees the soul as assisting consciousness in carrying out its healthy intuitive spiritual purpose.

Only people of integrity who can distinguish themselves from their mind and senses' "call of the wild" can lead us to real civilization. This is a call for a radical change in society, but in the face of our present situation of spiritual decay, there is no more noble an alternative. The respiritualization of society is essential, and ancient India's Vedic *varnashrama* system serves as a blueprint for the work at hand.

SPIRIT OF THE ENVIRONMENT

OUR PRESENT ENVIRONMENTAL CRISIS is in essence a spiritual crisis. Evidence of this has been documented in the well-known seminal work of Lynn White, Jr. His article, published in *Scientific American* in 1967, framed the ecological debate that gave birth to the field of environmental philosophy. As White irrefutably explained, we need only look back to medieval Europe and the psychic revolution that vaulted Christianity to victory over paganism to find the spirit of the environmental crisis.

Christianity's ghost-busting theology made it possible for man to exploit nature in a mood of indifference to the feelings of natural objects. It made the soul man's monopoly. This thinking went so far that in some quarters even women, man's better half, were considered soulless. Inhibitions to the exploitation of nature vanished as the Church took the "spirits" out of the trees, mountains, and seas.

This theory of the Church was more than an esoteric ideology. Translated into the practical, it fed more mouths and improved material comforts. With the wedding of science and technology blessed by the Church, there was no limit to how far man could go. Thus today's continued techno-scientific improvements on material nature are really no less than the Church's sustained witch-hunt that began in the Middle Ages. Deforestation, that is, has its roots in the uprooting of idolatry.

Yet White was as correct about Christianity's satanic role in taking the sacred out of nature as he was wrong about Eastern philosophy being incapable of offering a solution to the "Western" environmental crisis. White's prediction of an emerging Franciscan Christianity has not been taken very seriously, while Eastern philosophy has worked its way into the fabric of the American mainstream.

Taking the better part of White's debate, we can see from the ecocrisis we face today that misapplied spirituality can be very dangerous. It is perhaps more for this reason than that of cultural inappropriateness, as was White's formal argument, that he dismissed Eastern philosophy and Buddhism in particular. As a Christian, White may have been wary of the spirituality of Buddhism, yet as a scholar reluctant to speak about it. White's dismissal of Eastern spirituality was unfair, although his caution of misapplied spirituality appropriate.

Although Eastern philosophy does offer much to those interested in a spirituality that is environmentally sensitive, in many cases its influence in the West has amounted to a polar shift in spiritual thinking—from one extreme to another. A good example of this is the deep ecology movement. The term *deep ecology* first appeared in the 1970s in the writing of Norwegian philosopher Arne Naess, who was trying to create an environmental metaphysic. Deep ecology is now a well-known environmental movement with a political party popularly known as the Greens. The movement is often considered spiritual, and some of its members consider deep ecology their religion. Eastern philosophy has had a major impact on this movement, yet due to that influence the movement has done away with much of what is actually spiritual in the Western religious tradition. Deep ecology is a "spirituality" that is, in the traditional sense of the term, both soulless and Godless.

Thus I had reservations when I heard that deep ecology was a spiritual solution to the environmental crisis. Although I have a profound appreciation for the work that deep ecology is doing to improve the state of our natural environment, its loose definition of spirituality makes me as wary of it as

SPIRIT OF THE ENVIRONMENT

deep ecologists are of traditional Western religion. And if our environmental crises is essentially a spiritual one, a questionable spirituality cannot offer a complete solution.

Deep ecology's justification for redefining the spiritual is clear: traditional Western religion has brought us dangerously close to the destruction of our ecosystems. But how does deep ecology redefine spirituality? By adjusting spiritual to mean a lifestyle that does not bring humanity into conflict with nature. To take it a step further, a spirituality in which people see themselves as nature and nature as themselves—right livelihood and the void, as the Buddhists would say.

It is no wonder therefore that Buddhism is so popular within the ranks of deep ecologists. After all, traditionally speaking, it is a nonspiritual, nontheistic religion—a religion, that is, which lacks both God and soul. To quote scientist-activist Fritjof Capra, "Our Buddhism will be ecological awareness." Along with Buddhism, the religions of the Native Americans are popular and profound to deep ecologists, while from the traditional Western spiritual viewpoint Native American spirituality is primitive and pagan.

Maybe if the Greens ran the world spiritual culture would be thought of as much more than church on Sunday, for the Greens insist on a radical change in consciousness. But deep ecology falls short in the ultimate spiritual analysis. Is our spirituality reducible to a healthy ecosystem? Capra heralds this sorely mistaken idea thus: "Ecological awareness is ultimately a religious or spiritual awareness . . . the very essence of spiritual awareness."

For deep ecologists, animals, plants, and even inanimate objects have a right to live and have meaning and value beyond that which human society bestows on them. This outlook is certainly part of a spiritual vision, but spirituality does not stop there, as many deep ecologists think.

ANCIENT WISDOM

Deep ecology is an earthbound spirituality. For a new spirituality, it is strikingly similar to the pagan nature worship that Christianity sought to abolish. An old view with a new twist, it draws support for its thesis from James Lovelock's Gaia hypothesis. This is significant because the Darwinian evolution, as diametrically opposed as it is to the spiritual idea that consciousness is primary, is in Lovelock's words, "a key part of the Gaia theory." Deep ecology is a spirituality that is in many ways the antithesis of traditional Western religion. Man is no longer superior to nature; nature is superior to man.

Deep ecology is on one end of the spiritual spectrum, modern Christianity on the other. Neither seems to answer the need of the hour. Yet clearly the solution to the environmental crisis *is* the proper spiritual outlook. I would like to suggest a third idea that falls between the one extreme of Western traditional religion, which has ravaged our natural environment, and the other extreme of deep ecology, which, while saving the natural environment, has annihilated our soul. Let us look to the East, not to soulless Buddhism or Hinduism's popular monistic *Vedanta*, but to the theistic Vaishnava *Vedanta* of Sri Chaitanya. Sri Chaitanya's teaching offers elements found in traditional Western spirituality that are not found in deep ecology, and vice versa. His teaching also contains insights not found in either of these two world views. For example, his school posits a personal God with whom we can unite in service but never become, as does Christianity. This is a trait of Vaishnavism that is unique in Eastern spirituality. At the same time, Sri Chaitanya's teaching includes the doctrines of *karma*, reincarnation, and transcendence of duality, all of which are common to most Eastern spirituality. Unlike Christianity, Sri Chaitanya's creed does not offer man a monopoly on the soul, and it respects nature with awe, as deep ecology does.

SPIRIT OF THE ENVIRONMENT

Unlike both Christianity and deep ecology, Sri Chaitanya finds a higher harmony for man, nature, and a personal God.

Thus maybe we shouldn't be so quick to throw out the long-standing definition of spirituality that calls for a transcendence of material nature, distinguishes matter from spirit, and asserts a personal God. Nor should those of us who are Christians be so fearful of Eastern spirituality, which in the case of Vaishnavism, embraces a state of grace and a personal Godhead. Perhaps modern Christianity has merely misapplied these lofty ideas while deep ecology has misidentified them as the problem.

Must answering the clarion call to transcend material nature be synonymous with attempting to dominate her, as deep ecology proclaims? Is this merely an expression of the male ego? Is it a call of duality—nature versus humanity, the two pitted against one another? Does it *necessarily* lead to the breakdown of our ecosystems? Yes, as mistakenly applied in popular Western traditional religion. No, if we are speaking of the *dharma* of the soul as represented in the Bhagavat school of Sri Chaitanya.

The medieval *bhakti* renaissance in India paralleled Europe's "awakening" (the Renaissance), the precursor of the Industrial Revolution and the formal merger of God and reason, the divorce of man and nature. While European Renaissance and subsequent techno-scientific developments sealed the fate of humanity by declaring war on nature, the *bhakti* tradition brought us both transcendence and harmony with nature. A harmony with nature, fortunately, that is not at the cost of our eternal soul and individual spiritual ego, as is the price of deep ecology and its religious counterparts, popular Buddhism and neopaganism.

India's devotional renaissance was based on the *Bhagavat Purana*, the ripened fruit of the tree of Vedic literature. It was a revival of the spirit of devotion that flourished in India some five thousand years ago. The *Bhagavat* records the reign of pious kings who, properly spiritually aligned, ruled over their domain such that all—man and animal—lived in harmony with nature and God. Nature, pleased with the kings' temperament, provided all humankind's necessities in profusion. A reference from the *Bhagavat* to the reign of Maharaja Yudhisthira, one of the great heroes of the India epic *Mahabharata*, illustrates this beautifully: "The clouds showered all the water that people needed, and the earth produced all the necessities of man in profusion. Due to her fatty milk bag and cheerful attitude, the cow used to moisten the ground with milk. The rivers, oceans, hills, mountains, forests, creepers, and medicinal herbs, in every season paid their taxes to the king in profusion." Whether such Puranic records are historical accounts is another question, but they do at the very least represent the thinking of their time—that of reverence for nature. In this vision, humanity is the elder sibling of all other species. All species are products of material nature, humans included. Yet all living entities within these species are souls, and it is through the souls of humans conducting themselves in accord with the will of God that the individual souls of all species can be revived and a spirituality beyond the confines of material nature realized.

The *Bhagavat* is the natural progression from the more well-known *Bhagavad-gita*. The *Gita* instructs us that nature depends on God, and humanity depends on nature. Acts of devotion please Godhead, which causes nature to supply the needs of humanity. Thus there is an intimate relationship between God, humanity, and nature. The *Gita* instructs us that we must expand our sense of the environment and we must learn to tolerate it, however hostile or uncooperative it may seem: *tams titikshasva bharata*. The *Gita* advises us not to try to change the environment, improve it,

SPIRIT OF THE ENVIRONMENT

or wrestle with it. If it seems hostile at times, tolerate it. This does not mean that we should tolerate pollution of our water or the air. Here "environment" includes more than our natural surroundings. It refers to our life and experiences, which consist of actions and reactions *(karma)*, the shadows of our past actions. If we eat, we cannot complain about having to pass stool. So similarly, the *Bhagavat* teaches us that whatever happens to us we are the cause; we are to blame. Man proposes, God disposes. Yet in identifying ourselves as the culprit, we also find ourselves as the solution. In relation to the natural environment, this also applies. We are the cause of the sad state of the material environment, and we should try to change ourselves, our angle of vision, if we want to rectify the wrongs our natural surroundings suffer from as well as realize our spiritual destiny.

In the development of thought from the *Gita,* the *Bhagavat* announces that from tolerating that which comes to trouble us, we will eventually come to see that "the environment is friendly." If we tolerate what appears to be a hostile environment, we may eventually come to learn from it of the hostility within ourselves. Thus our environment can be our instructor, our well-wisher. With this vision, every grain of sand may be seen to be superior to ourselves. All of nature will be seen as a veritable guru, pointing in the direction of our spirituality.

The *rishis* of the *Bhagavat* school envisioned material nature in the light of its spiritual origin—consciousness. Thus with great respect they addressed the trees, mountains, stones, and the like as persons. But theirs was not a superstitious primitive theology. They perceived that all material manifestations are a shadow of the spiritual. They realized the fundamental basis of material reality to be consciousness and that consciousness is ultimately personal. While we see only the shadow and mistakenly accept it as the substance, they saw material nature as the shadow of the substance—consciousness. This is not nature worship, animism, or a soulless merger with matter, as found in the philosophy of deep ecology. It is a different idea altogether.

Deep ecology is fleeing from separateness and in search of wholism and oneness. It takes refuge in material nature. The Cartesian dualism of Christianity is unacceptable to deep ecology. The problem is that exclusive emphasis on oneness severely limits the scope of service, which Sri Chaitanya has described as the very *dharma* of the soul. The only way the mistaken notion that we are God, God is us, and all of us are nature can logically stand is if the so-called misperception of the *three* (God, humanity, and nature) is done away with, leaving only one. But in this vision, relationship (love and service) is mistakenly relegated to the realm of illusion, misperception. Service, in this theory, is part of illusion, not the ultimate reality. The potential for abuse of nature disappears with the loss of self, yet so does the potential for love. Without service, there can be no God to serve, no servant, and no love. Although deep ecology might argue that the oneness it seeks is that of an integrated whole in which the identity of individual parts is maintained in a system in which they are systematically integrated (material nature), still this leaves little room for love. It is rather a description of a process of material nature, which deep ecology thinks we are.

Cartesian dualism, on the other hand, separates God, humanity, and nature, isolating material nature from her spiritual origin. The price of this attempt to bridge God and humanity is the destruction of the natural environment. Thus exclusive emphasis on either of these polar opposites, oneness or difference, is unsatisfactory.

While wholism (oneness) is a necessary demand of our reason, individuality (difference) is an undeniable fact of our experience. The puzzle of the nature of the relationship between God, humanity, and nature cannot be solved without acceptance of both oneness and difference. Indeed, such a synthesis must be the desired goal of philosophy. Yet although a combination of these two is necessary, it seems impossible or inconceivable.

Thus the final test of human logic fails; what is logically necessary, is logically impossible. Sri Chaitanya's metaphysic of *achintya bhedabheda*, inconceivable, simultaneous oneness and difference, solves this problem. In Godhead there is no conflict between what is necessary and what is possible. His realm and the complete understanding of the nature of reality lie beyond the limits of human logic (thank God!). Thus, in reality, what is necessary, actually *is*, by the inconceivable *(acintya)* potency of Godhead. Humanity is one with God and nature, and different from them simultaneously.

The *Bhagavat* school distinguishes the soul from matter, yet both are considered feminine, *para prakriti* and *apara prakriti* respectively. Both are energies of the energetic. As heat and light are nothing but fire yet different from fire simultaneously, so the individual souls and matter are one with God and different from him at the same time. We are different in quantity yet one in quality with God. We can by his grace attain a perpetual state of oneness in purpose with him and rise beyond the duality of good and bad created by imperfect sense perception. When the individual soul aligns herself with Godhead, material nature comes to assist, for both are meant for the service of their source—Godhead, or *purusha*. Thus rather than a merger of humanity and nature, humanity and nature unite as maidservants of the *purusha*, Godhead.

This is a call for transcendence of the conception that humanity is the Lord of nature, yet it simultaneously distinguishes humanity and all life from matter and God. In the process, nature and ecosystems are understood and respected, for nature is not merely a fact, but has inherent value. Nature arises out of the spiritual plane of freedom, *Brahman*, and proper action within nature reinstates the individual soul in the freedom of transcendence.

Transcendence is not a struggle with nature, rather an appreciation of the purpose of nature as a servant of God. For those souls that want to rule instead of serve, nature shows a frown. But to those who care to serve her master, she smiles brightly. The purpose of nature is to shield her Lord from those not desirous of joining her in his service. It is not by fighting with her that we can achieve transcendence. Rather, absolute submission to her Lord puts us on her side and lifts her bewildering veil. This is a uniting with nature for a higher purpose of divine service, not a unification with nature as though material nature was all there is to life.

In human life the *jivatma*, or individual unit of consciousness, is capable of peeking out from beneath the blanket of material nature. When the soul acquires a human body, it has the proper vehicle from which to consciously disentangle itself from the maze of matter. To pull the cover of material nature over oneself again is a great mistake. To do so is to deny the prominent sense that tells us that we are different from matter, that we are consciousness. If we are but matter, from where does this sense arise?

This sense is not our false pride or material ego speaking to us. It is ourself. It is not proud to think ourselves different from matter. According to Sri Chaitanya, the *jivatma* is a tiny part and parcel of Godhead—a unit of service for the enjoyment of the whole. According to deep ecology on the other hand, we are not a part of nature—we are nature. And if nature is everything—God—well, so are our humble selves.

SPIRIT OF THE ENVIRONMENT

Sri Chaitanya taught a deeper humility, that of divine slavery. He taught that at the most fundamental causal plane only the sweet will of Krishna is operative. All movement therefore stems from his play. God is inviting us to play with him with every movement of nature. Thus Sri Chaitanya saw the transcendental will of Krishna manifest everywhere. Everything else, any other vision, was to him not the full picture. To see the world in this way is to find a higher harmony with nature and one's soul.

The authorized biography of Sri Chaitanya, *Chaitanya Charitamrta*, by Kaviraja Goswami, records Sri Chaitanya's journey from Bengal to Vrindavana. On this journey he passed thorough the great jungle Madhyapradesh (Jharikhanda). At that time, chanting the names of God, he caused species normally inimical to one another to embrace and chant with him. This is an important lesson to today's deep ecologists interested in interspecies communication. As for "harmony with nature," he exemplified something more—something spiritual.

Harmony with nature is a nice-sounding cliché, but is nature really in harmony? If it is, harmony for what? Unity sounds good, but unity *for what* is that which will determine the value of any harmony. The full picture of the harmony of nature can only be seen by understanding the movements of nature in relation to God's will. She has her service, as mentioned above. A prison, for example, is harmonious from the point of view of the government, but not from the point of view of the inmates. Nature is no doubt interconnected, wholistic, but the harmony of nature is one in which one living being is food for another. To put it in Darwinian terminology (he wasn't all wrong), "survival of the fittest."

To be in harmony with this reality in the eyes of deep ecology is to surrender to material nature. That is, surrender the "illusion" of our self, our soul. This is a kind of harmony, one similar to the Buddhist's *prakriti nirvana*. It is a kind of material *samadhi* in which the perception of separateness from the process of material nature, which is thought to be the cause of all material suffering, is eradicated. Although this may indeed eradicate suffering, it offers nothing positive in its stead. It is more or less spiritual suicide.

Sri Chaitanya offers much more. He has shown that a more meaningful and desirable harmony is one in which the struggle with material nature is terminated not by surrendering to her but rather by surrendering to the consciousness of Godhead behind the movements of nature. He sought to unite all souls, separated as we are by various material bodies and sense perception, and to awaken us to our spiritual prospect of unity in purpose with Godhead, which preserves a necessary element of divine service—individuality. The eradication of material suffering is a by-product of this divine culture; love of Godhead is its sweet fruit.

Although deep ecology rightly directs us to a change of consciousness, if we are serious about repairing the damaged state of the natural material environment, it leaves us at best with just that—a material environment. In steering us away from the traditional Western understanding of spirituality, it costs us more than we stand to gain. The price tag for its desired oneness with nature is certain essential elements of the Western spiritual heritage that are, in my perception, universal spiritual truths: the dignity of humanity as stewards of nature and all other species, a loving personal God, and our eternal soul. Sri Chaitanya on the other hand calls for a bigger picture—one in which all things, nature, humanity, and God exist in harmony. While deep ecology mistakenly tries to fit spirituality within ecology—even

SPIRIT OF THE ENVIRONMENT

to equate spirituality with ecology—Western religious tradition attributes no spirituality to nature whatsoever. Coming between the two, Sri Chaitanya correctly fits the common sense of caring for our natural environment within the culture of our spiritual lives. In his vision, nature cannot be divorced from her spiritual origin, and we must learn how to respect nature if we are to experience our spiritual destiny.

If we are interested in a spirituality that is environmentally sensitive, Sri Chaitanya's doctrine of divine love is well worth considering. It offers hope to all: that a life not only free from material suffering but full of divine love is before us. We need only change our angle of vision to live in this reality, one that material nature desires for us as well.

WHO DISCOVERED AMERICA?

IT VERY WELL MAY COME TO PASS in the near future that those concerned with truth will wrestle primarily with history rather than science. The obvious reason for this is that, in the words of Dr. Wilfred Cantwell Smith, author of *Theology and the World's Religious History*, "Humanity is more important than things. The truth about humanity is of a higher order than the truth about things."

History tells an intriguing tale, one that ultimately may provide the greatest support for a spiritual worldview. But history has also been distorted. An example of this is the "common knowledge" that Columbus discovered America. Some say he didn't, nor were any other Europeans the first to touch America's shores. There is good reason to reexamine the history of the world and the Americas in particular. An unbiased look into the development of our planet's civilizations may help to bring about a change in values, a shift from material values to spiritual ones.

What if Europe was really in darkness in comparison to the Far East and India that Columbus set sail to find? What if the popular idea that the Tibetans and the American Indians have much in common in terms of their spiritual culture is largely a result of another historical scenario? What if Hindus and Hopis, Advaitins and Aztecs, Tibetan monks and Mayans were part of one world culture—a spiritual one? Perhaps the development of Western civilization and the Protestant ethic, which many of the West are now coming to abhor, have gotten in the way of the spiritual development of humanity. Perhaps many technological developments, while making physical contact with other cultures more possible, have distanced us from one another in a deeper sense. Another historical scenario: The spiritually sophisticated Asians were the first to set foot on Western shores, and Asia, not Europe, was the seat of culture. The central focus of that culture was genuine spiritual development, not the mere shadow of the same in the form of the politically-motivated Pauline Christianity and later the Protestant ethic, which licensed humankind's exploitation of nature.

This theory is found in the Vedic literature of India. The ancient *Puranas* (literally, histories) and the *Mahabharata* make mention of the Americas as lands rich with gold and silver. Argentina, which means "related to silver," is thought to have been named after Arjuna (of silver hue), one of the heroes of that great epic. India's Puranic histories are, however, questionable to the rationalist. In the minds of the empiricists, they are more akin to myths. Yet myths have meaning, as the late Joseph Campbell has reminded us. The *Puranas* downplay in particular the mere recording of mundane events. The Puranic view is that even if its histories are only myths (which is not necessarily the case), the lessons to be learned from them are infinitely more valuable than what can be learned from recording the comings and goings of humanity. In their view, only those human events that serve to promote transcendental knowledge are worth recording. Although empiricists are justified in dismissing them from their viewpoint, the so-called myths and their followers are also justified in dismissing the empiricist's insistence that empirical evidence is final.

Granted, India has shown some lacking in her ability to record her story. But that is due to her preoccupation with the transcendent, the suprahistorical, and not to any ineptitude on her part. According to Kana Mitra in her article "Theologizing Through History?" "We [Hindus] tend to forget about history, and the deemphasis of *nama-rupa*—name and form [due to transcendent preoccupation]—

WHO DISCOVERED AMERICA?

is one of the reasons for not putting down a name or date in many of our writings. Consequently present-day historians have a difficult time in determining the date and authorship of various works."

Fortunately, for dealing with the "I'll-only-believe-it-if-I-can-see-it" mentality of the empiricist, there is considerable hard evidence and academic support for the Vedic theory that most people are unaware of. Unbiased consideration of this remarkable evidence may move modern-day rationalists to give serious thought to the more realistic spiritual outlook of "Only if you believe it can you see it." After all, reality is a living thing and it may reserve the right not to show itself but to those to whom it so chooses. Otherwise, why are we in illusion, or *in search* of reality? If it is something we can *attain* by our own prowess, how did we get here (in doubt) in the first place?

Many historians have scrutinized historical evidence to find more insight into the marvelous cultures that populated the American continent before Christopher Columbus was born. Their thirst for research was based on the assumption that the great Mayan, Aztec, and Incan civilizations could not have appeared all of a sudden in the Western world. Rather, they must have received strong influence from ancient Eastern cultures, mainly from India.

Alexander von Humbolt (1769-1859), an eminent European scholar and anthropologist, was one of the first to postulate the Asiatic origin of the Indian civilizations of the Americas. His and other scholars' views formed the basis for the "diffusionist" argument, which was opposed by the "isolationist" viewpoint. Diffusionists believe that the world's civilizations are a result of social contact (civilized man meets uncivilized man). Isolationists believe that civilizations cropped up all over the earth without physical contact with one another.

ANCIENT WISDOM

It is readily accepted that some twenty thousand years ago primitive Asians crossed the Bering Strait into North America and gradually moved south all the way to Tierra del Fuego, Argentina. Diffusionists maintained that after this occurred civilized Asiatic people distributed themselves via the Pacific, thereby bringing civilization to the Americas. Isolationists insisted that after the nomadic tribes crossed the Bering Strait, a homogeneous race of "Indians of the Americas" was formed, and the American tribespeople then went about reinventing all culture, duplicating in two thousand years what originally took about six millenniums in the Old World.

Henry Charlton Bastian, author of *The Evolution of Life* (1907), presented the concept of physiochemical evolution (*elementargedanke*), which gave strength to the isolationists. His theory advocated that the development of civilized man was a result of "a psychic unity of mankind," rather than social contact. Bastian's theory of *elementargedanke* influenced many anthropologists, and today, although the theory is not accepted, it is tacitly acknowledged as far as the conformities between America and Old World civilizations are concerned. This pseudo-evolutionist theory leaves much to be desired, and its unspoken acceptance casts doubt on the credibility of the anthropologists. After all, doesn't it tax our credulity when we are asked to believe that a whole series of complicated techniques like casting by the lost wax method, the alloying of copper and tin, the coloring of gold by chemical processes, weaving, and tie-dyeing and batik were by some miracle invented twice, once in the Old World and again from scratch in the Americas? What mysterious psychological law would have caused Asians and Americans to both use the umbrella as a sign of royalty, to invent the same games, imagine similar cosmologies, and attribute the same colors to the different directions?

WHO DISCOVERED AMERICA?

No archeologist today would attribute to prehistoric Europeans the independent invention of bronze casting, iron work, the wheel, weaving, pottery, writing, and so many other cultural elements that were derived from the Middle East. Similarly, the industrial developments in Britain were introduced from elsewhere within the European continent, not developed independently. What then would cause one to insist that what was not possible for the Europeans (duplicating culture independently) was possible for the American Indians? Especially when at the same time we are taught that the Europeans were of superior stock!

It was in 1949 that these opposing views met head-on at the Congress of the Americanists held in New York, which was sponsored by the American Museum of Natural History. At that time, the diffusionists presented an overwhelming mass of Asiatic-Pacific-American parallels. Nonetheless, much of the diffusionists' evidence continues to be ignored, and the isolationist view is more widely accepted. The reason for this may be more than empirical evidence or lack of the same. Indeed, it may be the faulty nature of the empirical approach, which depends on one's imperfect senses and causes one to dismiss facts that do not conform with the prevailing worldview.

The Aryan civilization of India is a logical choice for the beginning of the diffusion of our planet's civilization. American historian Will Durant, in his book *Our Oriental Heritage*, described India as the most ancient civilization on earth, and he offered many examples of Indian culture throughout the world. He demonstrated that as early as the ninth century B.C.E. Indians were exploring the sea routes, reaching out and extending their cultural influence to Mesopotamia, Arabia, and Egypt.

Although modern-day historians and anthropologists might prefer to accept Egypt or Babylon as the most ancient civilization, due to various archeological findings, their theories are by no means conclusive. The popular theory in the academic community that the Aryans were an Indo-European stock, who spoke an unknown pre-Sanskrit language and only later invaded India subsequently occupying her, is also considerably lacking in supportive evidence. Indeed, there is very little evidence whatsoever for the postulated Aryan invasion of India. But perhaps it is easier for modern people to accept ancient Egypt and Babylon, whose ancient civilizations have no living representation and thereby do not pose any challenge to the status quo.

But India is alive and kicking. Prominent traces of ancient Vedic civilization can still be found today not only in India but outside her borders as well. The life science of ayurveda, yoga and meditation, and Sanskrit texts translated into modern languages are all prominent examples. If we recognize ancient India as a civilized spiritual giant, we will have to reckon with her modern-day representations. It is altogether possible that the Vedic theory, if thoroughly researched, poses a threat to many of the concepts of modern civilization and the current worldview, as can be seen by the fact that the Vedic literature and spiritual ideology loomed as the greatest threat to the British in their imperialistic conquest of India.

The Aryans' footprints are found throughout neighboring Southeast Asia. They were skilled navigators and pioneers of many cultural developments. According to several sources, these Aryans ruled in Java, Bali, Sumatra, Borneo, Philippines, Cambodia, Vietnam, Annan, Burma, and Thailand until the fourteenth century. Even today, the kings of Thailand bear the title *Rama* after the Indian *Ramaraja* (the perfect kingdom said to have been governed by the incarnation of Godhead Ramachandra). And the story of *Ramayana* is depicted on the palace walls in Bangkok.

WHO DISCOVERED AMERICA?

Cambodia, the ancient Kamboja, boasts the largest temple complex in the world, named Ankor, from the Sanskrit language meaning "the capital city." It was built in the ninth century C.E. in honor of the Hindu god Vishnu. The complex extends over an area more than twice the size of Manhattan and took thirty-seven years to complete. Its physical and spiritual grandeur is found elsewhere only in ancient Greece, Egypt, and among the Mayan and Aztec civilizations. Cambodia's principle river is today called Me Kong, which some scholars say is derived from India's Ma Ganga (Mother Ganges).

Vietnam, once called Champa, figures prominently as a stepping-stone in the story of India's cultural expansion to the Americas. Furthermore, the Hindu state of Java was founded by the king of Kalinga (Orissa) in the first century C.E. Java is said to be the ancient Yava-Dveepa mentioned in the *Ramayana* and other Sanskrit texts. The Indonesian national flag flies the symbol of Garuda, the bird carrier of Vishnu. Garuda is also the national symbol of that country.

In 1949, two scholars, Gordon Ekholm and Chaman Lal, systematically compared the Mayan, Aztec, Incan, and North American Indian civilizations with the Hindu-oriented countries of Southeast Asia and with India herself. According to them, the emigrant cultures of India took with them India's system of time measurement, local gods, and customs. Ekholm and Lal found signs of Aryan civilization throughout the Americas in art (lotus flowers with knotted stems and half-dragon/half-fish motifs found commonly in paintings and carvings), architecture, calendars, astronomy, religious symbols, and even games such as our Parcheesi and Mexican *patolli*, which have their origins in India's *pachisi*.

Both the Hindus and the Americans used similar items in their worship rituals. They both maintained the concept of four *yuga* cycles, or cosmological seasons, extending over thousands of years, and conceived of twelve constellations with reference to the sun as indicated by the Incan sun calendar. Royal insignias, systems of government, and practice of religious dance and temple worship all showed remarkable similarities, pointing strongly to the idea that the Americas were strongly influenced by the Aryans.

Another scholar, Ramon Mena, author of *Mexican Archeology*, called the Nahuatl, Zapoteca, and Mayan languages "of Hindu origin." He went on to say, "A deep mystery enfolds the tribes that inhabited the state of Chiapas in the district named Palenque.... Their writing, and the anthropological type, as well as their personal adornments ... their system and style of construction clearly indicate the remotest antiquity.... [they] all speak of India and the Orient." Still another scholar, Ambassador Poindexter, in his two-volume 1930s treatise *The Arya-Incas*, called the Mayan civilization "unquestionably Hindu."

The Aztec culture in particular shows a striking resemblance to that of India. Aztecs divided their society into four divisions of both labor and spiritual status, as did the Hindus. In India, this system of government was known as *varnashrama*, or the division of society based on body types and mental dispositions resulting from past karma. As in Indian civilization, the Aztecs maintained a God-centered government in which people were employed in accordance with their natural karmic tendencies. The results of the labor of all the priests, administrators, mercantilists, and laborers were for the glorification of Godhead, who in turn was thought to provide for humankind.

Aztec boys were sent to school at the age of five, at which time they were put under the care of a priest and trained in various duties of temple life. The Aztec system of education bears a striking resemblance to the Indian sys-

WHO DISCOVERED AMERICA?

tem of *gurukula,* in which boys were sent to the care of a guru for spiritual and practical education. The Mayans and Incas had a similar approach to education, which was mainly a training for priestly service. Fanny Bandelier's translation of Sahagun's *History of Ancient Mexico* describes that the intellectually inclined boys were trained as "ministers to the idols."

Girls were educated in the domestic arts at home and did not mingle with young boys. Even as late as the 1930s, there was no courtship between Mexican Indian girls and boys, as is still the case in village life in India today. From conception to education, marriage, death, cremation, and even the observance of the *sati* rite, there are overwhelming parallels between Indian society and the Americas. Further evidence of cultural ties between the East and West is found in the statues of American gods who show a striking resemblance to the Hindu deities of Hanuman, Shiva, Indra, Vishnu and others. Such statues have been found throughout the Americas, and many of them can be seen today in museums in Central America.

The Mexican Indians and the Incas of Peru were primarily vegetarians. They were of high moral character and hospitable and generous as a habit. They practiced astrology, and mental telepathy was common among them. It was perhaps their peace-loving disposition that, like the Hindus, allowed them to be ruled by Europeans. Unfortunately, the American Indians did not survive their cultural exchange with Europe. The Europeans, through book burning and bayonet, successfully "converted" them, leaving very little trace of their noble civilization.

And what about Europe? When merchants sailing from India brought delicious spices, aromatic perfumes, incense, fine silk, precious stones set in delicate and rare jewelry, complex craftsmanship of ivory, and many other

ANCIENT WISDOM

goods never seen before by Europeans, the riches and mystique of that land captivated them. The stories told by many navigators about that land of wonder, where the palaces were built of varieties of marble rather than rush stone, decorated with beautiful sculptures and wooden inlay, made the Queen of Spain so covetous that she provided Christopher Columbus with all necessities for his famous journey. Columbus had heard of India's riches through the writings of Marco Polo. Polo had written that India "was the richest and noblest country of the world."

Europe, after Gutenburg's invention of the printing press, wasted no time in announcing the discovery of the New World. It was at this time that European historians began to present to the rest of the world that their land was the center of culture and civilization. In comparison to Indian society, however, the Europeans were rather crude. The ominous age of the Inquisition, with its persecution and fanaticism, the use of mechanical devices to insure the "chastity" of its women, the exploitation of the serfs, and self-destructive habits, such as indiscriminate eating and alcoholism within the higher classes, are all evidence of this. The original Palace of Versailles in Paris, although certainly a unique architectural creation requiring genius, was built without a single bathroom. Louis XIV and his court are said to have evacuated behind curtains, cleaning themselves with the same. The king was in the habit of substituting soap with Indian perfume and waited until his thirty-fifth birthday before he took his first complete bath.

When Europe was still uncivilized, Indian culture, as well as American culture, was highly advanced. When Europeans were still cave dwellers and nomads wandering from place to place subsisting through hunting, some American peoples were plowing fields and baking bread and dressing in cotton, the seeds for which came from India.

WHO DISCOVERED AMERICA?

The subtlety of Indian society, both eastern and western, marks its superiority to Europe. It was a subtlety of spiritual outlook that Europeans failed to appreciate.

The Industrial Revolution of Europe was prompted by India's cotton, which competed with European wool. Later when the popularity of cotton products imported from India increased, the Europeans began to manufacture cotton in mills. Thus it was even an Indian resource that prompted Europe's claim to fame—the beginning of modern technology.

Several ancient cultures of the Americas were more spiritually attuned than the Europeans. They also lived with great regard for nature. Many people today are searching out the spirituality of the Americas, a spirituality that was lacking in Europe and is now lacking throughout the world. The Christ's teachings were most certainly tainted with misunderstanding of that great savior's message of love. And he too is said to have been influenced by India's spirituality. His appearance in the world for that matter is mentioned in India's *Bhavisya Purana* long before the virgin birth took place.

The theory that India, Mother India, is the earthly source of spirituality can be to some extent supported by the fact that India is still today the most religious country in the world, with a theology that dates back to antiquity. The idea that she is the source of civilization as well, although supporting evidence is available, will ultimately require that modern man reevaluate what constitutes civilization before it gains wider acceptance.

SACRED COW

THE TERM *SACRED COW* HAS COME to mean any stubborn loyalty to something that impedes natural progress. The term originates in India, where the cow is literally worshipped while thousands of humans suffer from undernourishment. The common view of India in the West is that of an underdeveloped nation steeped in superstition.

Overpopulated, overcrowded, undereducated, and bereft of most modern amenities, India is seen to be a backward nation by "progressive" Western civilization. "If only India would abandon her religious superstitions and eat the cow!" Over several decades many attempts have been made by the "compassionate" West to alleviate "unfortunate" India's burden of poor logic and to replace her superstitions with rational thinking.

On the issue of India's sacred cow, much of the religious West finds common ground with the rationalists, with whom they are otherwise usually at odds. No doubt, worshipping God is one thing, but worshipping the cow while dying of starvation is a theological outlook much in need of reevaluation. The human race is said to have dominion over the animals, thus it would appear that the Indians have it backwards.

Popular opinion is not always the most informed opinion; in fact, this is usually the case. The many attempts to wean India from the nipple of her outdated pastoral culture have all failed. After two hundred years of foreign occupation by the British and many subsequent but less overt imperialistic attempts, we find that although India has changed, the sacred cow remains as sacred as ever. In all but two Indian states, cow slaughter is strictly prohibited.

ANCIENT WISDOM

If legislation were passed today to change that ruling, there would be rioting all over India. Despite considerable exposure to Western ideas, an Indian sage said, when asked what he thought of Western civilization, "I think it is a good idea. When will it begin?"

An unbiased look at the roots and philosophy of perhaps the longest-standing culture of the world may help us to see things a little more as they are—even about our own way of life. Sometimes we have to stand back to get the full picture. It is a natural tendency to consider one's own way the best, but such bullheadedness may cause us to miss seeing our own shortcomings. An honest look at the headlines of our hometown newspaper may inspire us to question exactly what it is we are so eager to propound.

Perhaps the most appalling aspect of the Western technological influence on India is found in the country's few "modern" cities. Bombay, Calcutta, Delhi, and other cities can be most frustrating to the average Westerner. Crude attempts at modernization are often worse than none at all. Although India's technology lacks the polish and sophistication of the West, its crude implementation nonetheless brings all of the adverse effects of a sophisticated form of the same amenities.

Real India is rural India. Village life accounts for the majority of India's population of seven hundred million and best illustrates the nation's ancient culture. The simplicity of India is often mistaken for ignorance, and her peacefulness mistaken for complacency. The serenity of Indian village life is overlooked or mislabeled by those who in the name of progress are really only operating under the axiom of "misery loves company." Perhaps the people of India live as they do for a good reason. Much of what goes along with Western "progress"—the mental anguish that causes us to do the most bizarre things and make many cities living hells—is relatively absent in India's rural lifestyle.

It is particularly difficult for Westerners to appreciate India's worship of the cow. After all, we live in the land of the hamburger. The American restaurant abroad is McDonald's. "Ole McDonald had a farm, did it ever grow!" Western economists often contend that killing and eating cows can solve India's food problems and lay a foundation for a lucrative export trade. This thinking has caused cow worship and cow protection to come under attack for centuries. Cow protection has been called a lunatic obstacle to sensible farm management.

India's cow is called the zebu, and an investigation of the controversy surrounding her brings us to the heart of village life in India. The average landholder in India farms approximately one acre. This is not enough land to warrant the purchase of a tractor. Even if the size of the land plots were increased to make the purchase of machinery cost-effective, India's unique weather, a five-season year including the monsoon, would quickly render the tractor useless. After the monsoons the soil is too soft for planting and must be quickly and efficiently prepared before the intense heat brings an end to the very short growing season. The loss of even one day considerably affects the overall yield. The zebu bullocks are ideal for they can easily plow the soft earth without overly compacting the soil as would heavy machinery.

Farming in India is a family affair. Their labor-intensive approach to cultivation involves everyone. This helps to sustain the family unit, which is sometimes considered to be the wealth of a nation. The staples of the Indian diet are grains: wheat and rice. Most of India is vegetarian. While the bull plows the field, helping to provide the grains, the cow supplies milk from which many dairy products are produced. Day after day, year after year, the cow and bull are the center of rural Indian life.

According to Frances Moore Lappe in her best-seller, *Diet for a Small Planet*, "For every sixteen pounds of grain and soy fed to beef cattle in the United States, we only get one pound back in meat on our plates. The other fifteen pounds are inaccessible to us, either used by the animal to produce energy or to make some part of its own body that we do not eat (like hair or bones), or excreted. Milk production is more efficient, with less than one pound of grain fed for every pint of milk produced. (This is partly because we don't have to grow a new cow every time we milk one.)"

If India, with its already strained resources, were to allocate acreage for the production of beef, the result would be disastrous. Advocates of modernization maintain that with the application of the latest farming techniques the yield of grain per acre would gradually increase, thus retiring the bullock from the field and putting him and his wife on the platter. Such advocates contend that with the introduction of beef into the Indian diet health would increase, thus furthering productivity. However, although India is far from being free of disease, its principal health problems are a result of urban overcrowding and inadequate sanitation and medical facilities. Whereas high blood pressure, heart disease, arthritis, and cancer (which are all linked to eating red meat) constitute the greatest health threats in the West, the Indian people are practically free from these afflictions. So the "fact" that India's health would increase with the introduction of beef into the diet is not likely to overcome the "superstition" of the people's religious beliefs that prohibit them from eating meat.

The religious beliefs of India are based on the *Vedas*, which constitute the most voluminous body of literature in the world. The *Vedas* and their corollaries deal elaborately with theism, describing many gradations of theistic thought. The idea that one should not eat meat, although central to Hindu philosophy, is only a secondary theme. To a large extent not eating meat only amounts to common sense and sensitivity. From this basis of sensitivity, an indicator of healthy consciousness, higher spiritual principles can be appreciated. The *Vedas* agree with the West's contention that man has dominion over the animals; however, the West's way of dealing with its dependents is revolting to Indians. After all, we have dominion over our children, and often elders as well, but would we be justified in slaughtering them for food? We become incensed if someone abuses even our dog!

The *Vedas* do not teach that the cow is superior to the human form of life and therefore worshippable. Rather, the *Vedas* teach that because the cow gives so much help to human society, she should be protected. The cow represents the sacred principle of motherhood. She symbolizes charity and generosity because she distributes her milk liberally. Her assistance frees the human race from much of the struggle of life, thereby providing more time for spiritual pursuits. Although modern technology may be said to do the same, it actually complicates life more and more and distracts from simple living and high spiritual thinking. We may become so mechanistic that we can fool ourselves into believing that cows or pets have no feelings.

India's critics have pointed out that although Indian village life may be simple, it is a marginal existence, a life of little surplus. If a farmer's cow turns barren, he has lost his only chance of begetting more bulls for the work team. And if a cow goes dry, the family loses its milk and butter. However, the situation is not as bad as technologically advanced people may think. In village life people are more interdependent. Helping one's neighbor is also considered

ANCIENT WISDOM

sacred. Sharing is commonplace. All of the father's male friends are affectionately referred to by the sons and daughters as "uncle" and all of the village women are seen as mother. Often the responsibility of caring for and nursing the young is shared by several mothers.

The heaviest criticism of the pastoral culture of India is that farmers insist on protecting even sick and aged cows. Western meat-eaters find this to be the height of absurdity. They think that such cows at least could be killed and eaten or sold. But the Indians think otherwise. Animal hospitals or nursing homes called *goshallas*, provided by government agencies or wealthy individuals in search of piety, offer shelter for old and infirm cows. This is thought to be a luxury that India cannot afford, as these "useless" cows are seen to be but competitors for the already limited croplands and precious foodstuffs. However, India actually spends a great deal less on their aging cattle than Americans spend on their cats and dogs. And India's cattle population is six times that of the American pet population. Would the same Western critics agree to feed their aging pets to the homeless?

Indian farmers see their cattle like members of the family. Since they depend on the cattle for their livelihood, it makes perfect sense both economically and emotionally to see to their cattle's well-being. Between harvests, the cattle are bathed and spruced up much like average Americans polish their automobiles. Special festivals are held in honor of the cow twice a year. These rituals are similar to Thanksgiving. Although the same in principle, there is a basic difference in the details of how we treat the turkey and how the more "primitive" Indians treat the cow.

India cares for over two hundred million zebus. This accounts for one-fifth of the world's cattle population. Critics say that if India does not eat her cows, the cows will eat India. Exasperated critics feel that even the cow is under-

SACRED COW

fed. However, in more recent years, India's critics have come to agree that the cow is essential to India's economy. Cattle are India's greatest natural resource. They eat only grass and generate more power than all of India's generating plants. They also produce fuel, fertilizer, and nutrition (milk) in abundance. India runs on bullock power. Over fifteen million bullock carts move roughly fifteen billion tons of goods across the nation. Newer studies in energetics have shown that bullocks do two-thirds of the work on the average farm. Electricity and fossil fuels account for only ten percent. Bullocks not only pull heavy loads but grind sugarcane and turn linseed oil presses. Converting from bullocks to machinery would cost an estimated thirty billion dollars plus maintenance and replacement costs.

The greatest energy contribution from cows and bulls is their dung. India's cattle produce eight hundred million tons of manure every year. The *Vedas* explain that cow dung is different from all other forms of excrement. Indian culture insists that if one comes in contact with the stool of any other animal, one must immediately take a bath. Even after passing stool oneself, bathing is necessary. But cow dung, far from being contaminating, possesses antiseptic qualities. This has been verified by modern science. Not only is it free from harmful bacteria, it also does a good job of killing them. It is as good an antiseptic as Lysol or Mr. Clean.

Most of the dung is used for fertilizer at no cost to the farmer. The remainder is used for fuel, leaving the world's fossil fuel reserves untouched. It is odorless and burns without scorching, giving a slow, even heat. A cook can leave pots unattended all day or return anytime to a preheated griddle. To replace dung with coal would cost India $1.5 billion per year.

Cow dung is used for both heating and cooling. Packed on the outside walls of a house, it keeps in the heat in the

ANCIENT WISDOM

winter and produces a cooling effect in the summer. And unlike the stool of humans, it keeps flies away and its smoke acts as a repellent for mosquitoes.

When technocrats were unable to find a workable alternative to the cow, they came up with a new argument for modernization. They suggested that the cattle culture be maintained, but in a more efficient manner. Several ambitious programs were initiated using pedigree bulls and artificial insemination, but the new hybrids were neither cheap nor able to keep pace with the zebus. The intense heat of India retired many of them well before old age. Although they produced more milk, this created additional problems, because there was no efficient system for distributing the surplus of milk throughout India's widespread population.

India's system of distribution is highly decentralized. It was thought that with bottling plants, pasteurization, and other sophisticated Western methods of distribution, all of India could have fresh, pure milk. Although the solution seemed simple, modernization again met its shortcomings. Behind the idea of setting up facilities for the distribution of milk, powdered milk, and cream was the expectation that in time people would begin to appreciate the abundant rewards bestowed by these new modern deities of technology, and cow worship would gradually disappear. But in the end it was modernization that failed to demonstrate its value.

Pasteurization proved to be a waste of time and money for Indians, who generally drink their milk hot, and thus boil it before drinking. With the absence of modern highways and the cost of milking machines and other necessities of factory dairy farming, imposing the Western dairy system on India was impractical; the cost of refrigeration alone would make the price of milk too expensive for ninety-five percent of India's population.

SACRED COW

After repeated attempts to modernize India's approach to farming—and in particular its attitude toward its beloved zebus—it became clear that these technological upgrades were not very well thought out. They were not to replace a system that had endured for thousands of years, a system not only economically wise but part of a spiritually rich heritage. It may well be time to export the spiritual heritage of India to the West, where the sacred cow of technology continues to threaten the progress of humanity in search of the deeper meaning of life.

RAGA AND ALL THAT JAZZ

SINCE THE MOST ANCIENT TIMES, music in India has been practiced as a spiritual science and art, a means to enlightenment. Only in recent years has India begun to lose her face of serenity and mystique, and it is no coincidence that such a departure from traditional spiritual values corresponds with the infiltration into India of pop music, heavy metal, and "cinema" songs. (Music makes us more than we make music.)

How ironic this is when at the same time the West is beginning to awaken to the sense of the sacred in music, primitive though such an awakening may be. That Indian music, more than any other influence, has been most instrumental in this shift of Western consciousness only adds to the irony.

It is a sorry sight to see—rather, hear—the U.S. Top Ten blaring even in some of the most remote villages of a land of rich spiritual heritage (especially when the songs are "adapted" for the Hindu audience!). But still in India today there are many places where music and self-realization are wedded in a harmony that makes one weep and search within for a deeper meaning to life. *Bhajana, kirtana,* and classical Indian music all play upon sympathetic strings within the hearts of our souls, drawing us out from behind the curtain of illusion.

What a surprise it must be to the Indian student, allured by the loud voice of the Western material success ethic, to leave his or her village and cross the ocean to find that many fellow Western students are looking eastward—knowingly or unknowingly—toward a holistic worldview, which is so typical of Eastern philosophy. Eastern influence on Western

ANCIENT WISDOM

society has been immense yet characteristically subtle over the last twenty-five years, and the field of music is no exception.

America's beat generation of the '50s and early '60s, followed by the hip generation of the '60s and '70s, took popular music, rock, and jazz from being a sensual experience to an intellectual one, bordering sometimes on the spiritual, but not without foreign influence. The medium of music cannot but propel humanity in the spiritual direction, however far we may digress from that course for some time. From the bottom there is nowhere to go but up, and the West has bottomed out musically in the twentieth century, which marks only a short detour from the world's musical heritage. After all, only a century past, Western music was clearly spiritually oriented, some well-known examples being the works of Bach and Beethoven.

Of all kinds of music through which a spiritual urge might surface, jazz may seem the most unlikely. A brief history of jazz followed by a look at the background of Indian *raga* will clearly illustrate the apparent unlikelihood of these two being anything more than uncommon bedfellows. But it was through jazz that Indian music and spiritual yearning first sang out in America. The background of the consciousness behind these two forms of musical expression, jazz and Indian *raga*, are diametrically opposed. In this sense no two musical forms are further from one another. Yet it is the very underlying spirit of music in general that dictates their union. The spirit inherent in musical expression is humanity searching for fulfillment in life. Thus the musical urge may ultimately be seen as a spiritual one, though it is all too often misdirected in modern times.

Jazz first appeared on the American music scene in the French Quarters of the then notoriously shady New Orleans. Imported from Africa via the Caribbean (Haiti)

RAGA AND ALL THAT JAZZ

with slave trade, jazz has its roots in the musically complex, spiritual vacuum of voodoo rhythm. Although voodoo rituals were once illegal, they nonetheless sustained an influence in the United States in New Orleans, where as late as 1835 they were practiced. Such practice included animal blood sacrifice. There is no dissenting opinion among musicologists that such African drum rhythms evolved through blues and ragtime into the basis for jazz.

Many consider Buddy Bolden the founding father of jazz. Bolden took his music to the streets of New Orleans in the 1890s. His music appealed primarily to those of ill repute who frequented the city's red light district. It was there that jazz's founding father cultured a heavy drinking habit and contracted syphilis, from which he was eventually driven insane and committed to a state institution to die an inglorious death in 1931. The pattern of his life was expected of those who had a thirst for this kind of music.

From the brothels of New Orleans, jazz spread throughout the country, finding an audience amid the lowest sections of society. The word *jazz* first appeared in print in 1917 in a New York newspaper. There it was described as a "syncopated riot." As its influence spread, it came under attack from the press. According to pro-jazz writer Frank Tirro in his book *Jazz: A History*, in the early '20s "jazz became the symbol of crime, feeblemindedness, insanity, and sex." It was not until the repeal of prohibition, a short-sighted economic concession to immorality, that jazz, along with liquor, came into "respectability."

With the fears of sharp moralists put aside under the banner of progress, the rhythms of jazz soared into popularity until it bowed to its successor, rock 'n roll. During this transitional period when, under the influence of Miles Davis, jazz took on an intellectual tone separating it from early rock, the influence of Indian music and its spiritual

ANCIENT WISDOM

consciousness first appeared in jazz. This was the spawning of the interest that we find today in America's alternative culture for rediscovering the sacred in music. The cornerstone musician in the jazz world to this unlikely bridge from the utterly material jazz wasteland to the spiritual landscape of India was John Coltrane.

Although there are musical similarities between jazz and *raga* (which we will discuss later), the consciousness behind their origins are like the difference between night and day. Listening to Indian music requires that we hear with our hearts, for the entire orientation of classical Indian music is toward the mystery of the soul. Often before Indian performers begin their performances, they will instruct the audience in the art of listening as the artists have been instructed from their mentor.

The degree of discipline to which the student of music is expected to adhere is considerable. Purity and piety are foremost in every endeavor. Once in West Bengal I observed a very young boy playing an indigenous clay *mridanga*, or *khol*. I asked him what was the most important thing to know if one was to become proficient in playing the drum. To my surprise he spontaneously replied, "the *mantra*." Then he recited a beautiful verse in praise of the drum, bowing his head to the instrument. It was as though he conceived of himself as a servant of the drum, rather than the drum an object of his subjective experience. In reality we are all instruments in the hands of the divine, and those things that assist us in realizing this fact should be held in reverence.

Ravi Shankar's description of his life as a disciple of spiritual music underscores this point. His practice would begin at 4:00 A.M. After two hours he would bathe and do his morning spiritual practice. Shankar stated that "total humility and surrender to the guru" were expected; "a complete shedding of the ego" was the goal. Shankar further stated, "The only entertainment I had was going on long walks along the river or the lovely hillside." Clearly, music was not entertainment to Ravi Shankar but a spiritual force.

About the musical culture of India's ancients, Shankar says,

> There is no dearth of beautiful stories relating how great musicians and saint-musicians such as Baiju, Bavare, Swami Haridas, or Mian Tan Sen performed miracles by singing certain *ragas*. It is said that some could light fires or the oil lamps by singing one *raga*, or bring rain, melt stones, cause flowers to blossom, and attract ferocious wild animals—even snakes and tigers—to a peaceful, quiet circle in a forest around a singing musician.
>
> To us in this modern, mechanical, materialistic age, all this seems like a collection of fables, but I sincerely believe that these stories are all true and that they were all feasible, especially when one considers that these great musicians were not just singers or performers, but also great yogis whose minds had complete control of their bodies. They knew all the secrets of *tantra, hatha yoga*, and different forms of occult power, and they were pure, ascetic, and saintly persons. That has been the wonderful tradition of our music.

Legends abound in the annals of India's music, attesting to the extraordinary prowess of India's devotional musicians. We may have difficulty believing some of the things we hear about them, but the difficulty may lie within

ANCIENT WISDOM

ourselves. We have a tendency to measure everything with respect to our own experience, limited as it is. Proud of our modern scientific and technological achievements, we may be blinded from ever discovering anything that is really new. By this I refer to the spiritual dimension, the plane of dynamic living where everything is ever-fresh and ever-lasting. The world of the physical senses—where most of humanity is imprisoned—is rather a stale affair. Those of us who are controlled by our passions will never know the truth of the spiritual dimension. Could the *rishis* of India's past perform "miracles" through their music? One might answer rhetorically: *Is anything really "impossible"?* Need we continue, in Napoleon's words, to refer to a "fool's dictionary" as we approach the twenty-first century?

Even within the hackneyed material realm of the five elements (earth, water, fire, air, and ether), modern material science deals only with the first four elements in almost all their achievements. The manipulation of sound in space is an even more refined material science yet unknown to today's technocrats. Western psychic Edgar Cayce predicted that the medicine of the future will be sound. Certainly, we will have to refer to the *rishis* of the past as this day approaches. Perhaps by that time the sense of our present progress will be put in proper perspective. It seems almost silly to ask if sound can influence our consciousness, but when we speak of powerful examples of this from the past, most gawk in disbelief. There is no doubt that with the advancement of material science we will come to appreciate the power of sound and music, but if we are to get the most from any of our "discoveries," we must change our angle of vision. We must see *ourselves* as instruments and tune ourselves to the symphony of the divine.

This is very different thinking from the thinking that lies behind materialistic music such as jazz. Thus it seems

RAGA AND ALL THAT JAZZ

reasonable to contend that a marriage between jazz and *raga* must be based on technical musical similarities.

Indian music has always placed emphasis on vocal expression over instrumental. The best instrumental is thought to be that which renders most faithfully the subtleties of the human voice. Jazz is often also conceived of vocally, even purely instrumental jazz. Indian classical music is *melodical*, whereas Western music is *harmonical*. Music of the world began as a melodic stream, which later branched out into harmonics. Although Indian musicians knew the principles of harmony, they chose to develop their systems along the lines of melody: one-line, or one-dimensional, "horizontal" music, which lends itself to meditative individual expression. Here we find a similarity to jazz, which gives a license for long solo improvisation.

Because Indian music is modal, it knows no change of keys but sticks to one steady ground note. Very important to Indian music are embellishments, tone colors, and intervals that do not exist in well-tempered Western music, which allows expression *only* through improvisation. Jazz is also modal, and it does not limit itself to the tones of Western tuning. In theory Indian octaves consist of sixty-six microtones, but in practice there are twenty-two tones per octave, which is nearly twice the number found in the Western octave. In many freestyle jazz improvisations, one can also find the use of this many tones.

The rhythmic possibilities of India's music have been attractive to jazz musicians. Trumpeter Don Ellis was one of the first to emphasize the similarities between jazz and Indian music. In *Jazz* he wrote, "Jazz musicians like to think of themselves as masters of rhythm (and in comparison to European music they are in the forefront), but . . . how crude and primitive the conventional jazz musician's grasp of rhythm is in comparison with Indian music. . . . Any jazz

ANCIENT WISDOM

musician who desires to really acquire a grasp of rhythm should, if at all possible, study Indian music."

Indian music is played with a much different conception of time than Western music. Sometimes one piece can last an entire night. In his *The Jazz Book,* Joachim-Ernst Berendt has demonstrated that "a non-Western concept of time plays a decisive role in jazz." According to Berendt, "Jazz is played with two different concepts of time, one Western and one non-Western."

A composition or melody in classical Indian music is called a *raga* or in the feminine, *ragini*. *Raga* means that which gives pleasure. *Ragas* and *raginis* are formed by the combination of the seven basic notes on the scale: SA, RE, GA, MA, PA, DHA, and NI. Each *raga* and *ragini* is considered to be a person. The *rishis* perceived that behind everything is personality; consciousness has personality. The *ragas* are also associated with a particular time of day and often to a particular season. Within the guidelines of the *raga* system, musicians uniquely express themselves. In India over the centuries, there evolved almost six thousand different *ragas*. The system is an extremely flexible one, as is jazz among the rest of Western music.

Ragas combine everything that Western music breaks down into theme, key tuning, phrasing, form, and even composition. But they are not thought of as compositions by their would-be musical composers. According to Ravi Shankar, a *raga* is "discovered as a zoologist may discover a new animal species, or a geographer may discover a new island." They are better understood as musical archetypes.

Raga is accompanied by rhythmic time cycles. These time cycles are known as *matra* and can be as long as 108 beats. Although the Western ear is lost, the trained ear is following with a subtle excitement the longer sequences, waiting for the rhythmist to complete the cycle and meet with the other musicians, who have all moved apart in subdivisions of intricate rhythmic elaborations. Imagine 1, 2, 3, 4/1, 2, 3, 4. Now try 1, 2, 3, 4 . . . 105, 106, 107, 108/1, 2 . . .! It is no wonder that jazz musicians were interested in borrowing from this system.

But with all of these similarities, it must be underscored that Indian music is vastly different from jazz. Its rhythms do not agitate sensual urges as jazz does, but quiet them, opening us to the voice of divinity within. Therefore, although many jazz musicians may have initially attempted to utilize Indian *ragas* for their own material purpose, many musicians became affected by this spiritual music and subsequently by the entire culture and philosophy of spiritual India.

If something is really spiritual, it cannot become contaminated; rather, contaminated things become purified when in touch with that which is absolutely pure. Just as the sun is not affected by any amount of the contaminated water it evaporates but turns it into distilled water, so the truly spiritual can only "spiritualize" that which is material. This is not to say that all Indian music is absolutely spiritual, but it is *all* light years ahead of jazz. Why then, one might ask, are Indians today becoming attracted to the worst of Western music, as has been alluded to earlier on? As a whole they are not, but the powerful influence of Western propaganda has certainly taken its toll upon Indian youth, who do not always avail themselves to their country's great spiritual and cultural heritage. And why is India so underdeveloped materially? We must remember that material progress is certainly not a requirement for spiritual evolution, and in many instances it has been seen to hinder a nation's spiritual growth.

Other than the technical similarities between jazz and *raga* that attracted jazz musicians to Indian music, there are

ANCIENT WISDOM

other sociospiritual explanations for this odd coupling. As worldly as jazz is, as affirmed by its own advocates who have been known to refer to it as the "down beat," there is an up side to this music from the spiritual point of view. Jazz lyrics, which are instrumentally mirrored, are focused on some themes that are characteristic of spiritual seeking.

Jazz often highlights the impermanence of human relationships, a spiritual fact of life. Jazz musicians may not have known what to do about it, but at least they recognized it and sang about it, while most others sang sentimentally in other musical genres about how good things really are, when in fact, objectively speaking, they are not. Jazz musicians saw the down side of life and the masquerade of the "well off." The suicidal urge that appears in jazz and blues may from the purely transcendental outlook contain within it some understanding of the utter futility of material existence, albeit lacking a spiritual solution.

The wandering theme of jazz is also one that is found in the lives of saints, who want to avoid becoming attached to any particular place. There is a wisdom in the down-and-out and an openness as well to alternative thought. Until one realizes how bad material life is, heading in a purely spiritual direction will be difficult. This assessment of jazz may seem to be reaching when it is also a fact that other themes within jazz are obviously demoniac and destructive, but not everyone on skid row belongs there. Many people "go down" to "go up." The lack of practical spiritual insight in the world may be a primary cause for the downfall of many intelligent people who, without such insight, do not know where to turn with their justifiable frustration.

Whatever the reason, be it the technical similarities between jazz and *raga*, the latent spirituality in the jazz mindset, or simply the grace of the divine that knows no reason, jazz was the musical medium through which Indian music and its spirituality chose to make itself known to the West. From record producer Dick Bock's 1957 collaboration with Ravi Shankar to his 1961 recording of Shankar with flutist Bud Shank to Paul Horn's meditative music, the sounds of India made their way into the ears of America.

There were many musicians who became caught up in the mystery of Indian music, and of course the beat '50s poets as well, but of all of them, John Coltrane played the highest note. Coltrane is perhaps the best example of how India's spiritual vibration affected jazz musicians spiritually. Coltrane's life was deeply moved by Indian spiritual thought, as were those with whom he played. His albums, beginning as early as 1961 with *India*, followed by *Meditations: A Love Supreme*, and *Om*, are examples of this influence on his music. His meditation practices and his own words speak of his transformation: "I have had experience, by the grace of God, a spiritual awakening, which has led me to a richer, fuller, more productive life." In the very least, he began to move in the direction of spiritual India.

According to Ralph Gleason, the late San Francisco art critic, Coltrane shifted the consciousness of America's youth from the United States to Asia, no small feat. This new influence extended beyond jazz to rock and pop music, and more so into the very way we think as a society. As our musical focus shifted, so did our lives, however slightly, in the spiritual direction. It is not that this historical period of change was by any means entirely spiritual, but there is no doubt that spiritual influences of Eastern philosophy made their way into our lives largely through the musical medium beginning with jazz.

Along with the introduction of Indian classical music into Western society came the seed forms of Indian music as Indian gurus brought *mantras* and chants to the streets of the United States. The popular Hare Krishna *mantra* was heard for months over the radio within ex-Beatle George Harrison's number one single "My Sweet Lord." Many may have thought nothing of it, but it is safe to say that it had its impact.

It is from these roots that the present "new age" movement has its beginnings, although many who consider themselves "new-agers" may not realize it. There is, however, not a single new age musician who does not recognize the powerful spiritual influence of Indian music and *mantra*. Stephen Halpern, sometimes called the founding father of new age music, has said, "John Coltrane was one of my ideological patron saints. His album *A Love Supreme* changed my life and opened me up to the possibility that music could bring me into higher states of consciousness." Just how spiritual new age music is, or even how musical it is, is a subject of debate; but so was the music of the great classical composers at one time. However, one thing is sure: the sentiment behind new age music—that of wanting to rediscover the sacred power inherent in music—is our yellow brick road en route to Kansas.

Hardly have we become spiritualized as a society as a result of all this. Neither are there very many individuals who are *experiencing* spiritual life as it is described by the *rishis* and in the *Vedas* and *Upanishads*. A "new age" may not be about to dawn at any moment, but the fact that a number of people are at least seeking deeper meaning in life—and in relation to our topic, seeking the sacred in music—is encouraging. Perhaps if we look more deeply into the roots of this new-found outlook (one that is a radical departure from the musical direction we have been heading in for the last century) toward the spiritual heritage of ancient India, we will be better equipped to move practically, rather than wishfully, toward transcendence.

RAGA AND ALL THAT JAZZ

In India, as the whisper of the *Upanishads* is drowned out by heavy metal, and Indian youths become enamored by the false promise of materialism, many from the West are looking eastward for new direction. Perhaps through the power of spiritual music that knows no boundaries the concepts of East and West will be broken down, and ever so gradually people of all castes and creeds will rise to the symphony of pure spirituality.

KNOWLEDGE OVER NESCIENCE?

THE DOG IS RUNNING

ON FOUR LEGS AND BARKING.

MODERN HUMANITY

IS RIDING ON FOUR WHEELS

AND BLOWING ITS HORN.

IS THERE ANY CATEGORICAL

DIFFERENCE BETWEEN

THESE TWO?

THE CASE FOR CONTINENCE

AS CONSCIOUS BEINGS WE HAVE the capacity to create life through our sexual energy. This is, of course, in a relative sense only. Creators we may be, yet only as instruments, for on the macrocosmic scale, life's origins can be traced to an ultimate spiritual cause.

If we consider the origin of all life divine, it is natural to think of our own microcosmic part in creation as a sampling of the work of divinity. Therefore, it follows that the sexual fluids of procreation are an extremely valuable commodity.

The emergence of a new ethic, "the preservation of the planet," has caused many to adopt the paradox of "freedom through restraint." For example, recent legislation curtailing smoking in public suggests that people are becoming more conscious that the freedom to breathe fresh air requires that we refrain from smoking. Many of us now refrain from ingesting highly processed foods jam packed with preservatives that are good tasting but life taking. Similarly, it may be time to consider retaining the sexual fluids within us that are life giving. This will require tremendous restraint, yet may result in an unprecedented sense of freedom. Perhaps it is time to reconsider continence, a long-forgotten virtue of days gone by.

The concept of continence presented herein is not a wholesale advocacy of complete abstinence from sexual indulgence. Rather, it is a well-rounded approach to sexual freedom. The first wave of the sexual revolution promoted only a one-dimensional view of sexual expression—genitally-centered, orgasmic sexuality. The case for continence promotes a heightened regard for the sexual

ANCIENT WISDOM

energy that lies within us. It draws attention to the multi-dimensional nature of sexual energy. Not only is our sexual energy the source of the highest sensual experience (its most limited aspect), but it is the source of procreation, optimum health, increased mental and intellectual capacity, and mystic experiences. Moreover, complete understanding of sexual energy leads to the ultimate spiritual experience.

Progress requires acceptance and elimination. Life is like a great ladder consisting of many steps. We have to be more concerned with reaching the top than with any particular step. At one point acceptance of a particular idea may constitute progress. Later that same idea may have to be eliminated in order that we remain progressive. To let go of the first step enables us to ascend on the ladder of life. Yet for many the ascent beyond one-dimensional sexuality may seem nearly impossible and perhaps unnecessary. I will raise some very practical points that show how, by changing some of our habits and the way we think of ourselves, continence (the impossible) becomes plausible. I will also discuss the advantages of embracing continence, either in relationship with our life's partner or as a single person, for continence can help us in our progress in the physical, intellectual, and spiritual dimensions.

The gross sexual urge is both natural and formidable. The urge is so strong that we seldom entertain the thought of curtailing it. Yet in keeping in harmony with nature there are several points to consider. Although it is obviously true that the sexual urge is natural, the extent to which we are one-dimensionally absorbed with it is unnatural. Bypassing the broader scope of the emotional need for relationship and dealing only with the gross act of sex itself, it is apparent that we *can* live without it. In comparison, other natural biological needs, such as eating and evacuating, can never be given up. By nature's arrangement, there

THE CASE FOR CONTINENCE

is no scope for sexual indulgence during childhood or old age.

There are cycles for all species during which the sexual urge heats up, and it is at this time that the female is most fertile. By nature's arrangement, sex and reproduction go hand in hand. In consideration of this, contraception, an invention of humanity, appears rather unnatural. We proclaim ourselves animals of reason. But it is questionable just how rational an animal we really are, when sexual indulgence outside of procreation seems to be our norm. Of course, animals also indulge in masturbation, and other sexual acts outside of procreation (although rarely). But they are, after all, animals without reason. Reason dictates that our sexual preoccupation is unnatural. Although it may *feel* natural enough, such feelings may be largely prompted by external influences.

Although Freudian psychology attempted to present a nonmechanistic explanation of the sexual urge, its explanation grossly neglects certain physical considerations. If we examine some physical causes for sexual desire, we will find a natural way of decreasing gross sexual activity. For example, there is considerable evidence to support the idea that diet influences sexual desire. The diet that people keep is often unnatural—determined by the demands of the fastidious tongue rather than nutrition.

In *The Better Way*, Issac Newton makes the following statement: "They who have ever carefully noted the effects on themselves of most kinds of alcoholic stimulants, of coffee, oysters, eggs, spices, and excess of animal food of most any kind . . . cannot surely with justice charge upon 'nature' the exuberance of their amatory desires."

Many civilizations of the past, such as the Orphics, Pythagoreans, Essenes, Gnostics, neo-Platonists, and Manichaeans, practiced continence with a view to achieve

ANCIENT WISDOM

optimum health and spiritual regeneration. All of them held that for the practice of continence to be successful, one must maintain a vegetarian diet. Pythagorus, Plato, Aristotle, St. Theresa, St. Francis of Assisi, Spinoza, Newton, and later Gandhi and Tolstoy, to name a few, all practiced continence with the help of vegetarianism.

Today of course there are an increasing number of people becoming vegetarians. The arguments in support of this diet are overwhelming. They include medical, ethical, economical, and spiritual considerations. On all fronts the vegetarian movement is going forward, held off only by obstinacy and the need of a proper vehicle to make its ideals known everywhere. Vegetarianism is a giant step in the direction of world transformation. Such a vegetarian worldview could also provide impetus for a continent lifestyle to catch on.

Of all foods meat, and beef in particular, is the most potent aphrodisiac. Along with meat, fish and eggs produce a similar effect—sexual excitement. The testes, when well filled with sperm, stimulate the sexual sensory centers. The heads of the sperm consist chiefly of nucleoproteins. Foods rich in protein, when absorbed in the diet, influence the sperm to cause sexual excitement. Of course people accustomed to a diet consisting of these kinds of foods will not be able to identify them as the source of their sexual arousal. Yet if they refrain from meat eating for a short time, they will notice that their sex desire decreases.

A high protein diet of meat, fowl, fish, and eggs is also high in uric acid. Coffee, tea, and chocolate also contain uric acid, as well as caffeine and other toxic alkaloids that are sexually stimulating. Caffeine increases the heartbeat, raises the blood pressure, and thus serves as an aphrodisiac, while uric acid causes inflammation of the genital mucus membrane that is the seat of sexual sensitivity. In women an acid-forming diet causes inflammation of the uterine mu-

THE CASE FOR CONTINENCE

cus membrane and tends to promote the occurrence of leukorrhea and increased menstruation.

Tobacco is another powerful aphrodisiac. Men who work in tobacco factories often experience increased nocturnal emissions. This is the result of tobacco's irritating effect on the genital mucous membrane. Tobacco can also create havoc in the female reproductive system, producing sterility and cancer of these organs.

All the above-mentioned stimulants have a strong influence on the blood. Toxic blood caused by stimulants coupled with the toxic effect of poorly digested food irritates the nervous system and especially the extremely delicate nerves that govern reproduction. Through the nervous system, with the help of the brain, passions are aroused.

Adopting a vegetarian diet and eating alkaline rather than acid-producing foods will counteract uric acid formation and reduce sexual inclinations. The secret to sexual control for men lies in maintaining the blood and urine in as alkaline a state as possible so as not to irritate the sexual centers in the mucus lining of the prostatic utricle. This state is best achieved through a low protein diet. Vegetables that contain large quantities of fiber and water, such as cabbage, turnips, beets, and carrots, and fruits like melons are helpful in this connection. Potatoes are very alkaline and among grains rice is lowest in uric acid content. In general, a low protein diet is the best diet for pursuing continence.

Thus by the mere changing of our diet we may find that the impossible becomes plausible. We have to remember that most Americans thrive on meat, fish, and eggs, and between meals pay considerable attention to other stimulants, such as coffee, tea, and cigarettes. Along with our sexually stimulating habits, we are constantly bombarded with sexually explicit advertising, in which men and women are often depicted as nothing more than sexual objects. Sex is on our minds, to say the least. Naturally, the average person will cringe at the thought of sexual abstinence, but have they stopped to consider the fact that they are practically *living* on sexual stimulants?

A healthier diet and freedom from smoking and intoxication are positive in and of themselves and are also integral parts of a continent lifestyle, yet there are still other positive benefits that result from recycling our sexual energy. Hearing about these benefits makes continence even more plausible. While improving our overall health, continence may also be a solution to major social dilemmas that threaten humanity. A continent lifestyle also aids intellectual growth and contributes indirectly to spiritual development, without which true continence is not possible.

In light of continence and the emerging ethic of planetary preservation, there are several modern day dilemmas worth mentioning. The AIDS epidemic, the threat of overpopulation, and the seemingly endless debate surrounding abortion are all issues that could be practically solved by continence.

While I write, the headline in the San Francisco *Chronicle* reads, "AIDS State of Emergency Sought." If there is a state of emergency, we should be prepared to consider any positive proposal aimed at bringing about a solution. A public education program is already in place with government funding. This is the most complete remedy at hand. Education generally takes precedence as the optimum long-range solution to any problem. I am suggesting this education focus on continence because over the centuries the ancients and the wise have extolled the virtues of a continent lifestyle. Courses on continence would revolutionize our present one-dimensional sex education. The present program has no scope for penetrating to a deeper understanding of the nature of our sexuality. Such limited, one-dimensional education may prove to be counterpro-

THE CASE FOR CONTINENCE

ductive. To a large extent (through advocacy of contraception) it serves to *promote* genital, orgasmic sexuality, which, ironically, may lead to the breakdown of our overall health, including the immune system!

With the development of sexual energy in youth comes maturation, which includes physical maturation. Modern-day Western psychosexual theories consider only the physical body however. This model is a closed system, which doesn't take into account the subtle body or consciousness. For example, this model suggests that periodic discharge of semen is necessary after one reaches maturity. On reaching maturity, in this model, there is no longer an internal need for the semen. Although this is a popular conception that promotes genital sex, it is by no means the unanimous opinion within the scientific community.

In another model, which considers higher realities, an alternative use for sexual energy arises. The popular Western model is in line with the "throwaway society" we live in. Our second model, a spiritual one, calls for a recycling of the sexual energy, which creates a greater balance in body ecology. This results in increased mental and physical vitality. In this model there is also scope for transmutation of sexual energy, which is necessary for higher psychic development.

Sexual fluids when retained increase overall vitality. Any male athlete is afraid of untimely nocturnal emission the night before a match. Sexual contact is often prohibited for women and men alike during athletic training. Overall, it is reasonable to propose that semen, which is instrumental in cell reproduction, when retained will serve to produce and generate vitality within.

Gandhi wrote, "The horror with which ancient literature regarded the fruitless loss of the vital fluid was not a superstition born of ignorance . . . Surely it is criminal for a man to allow his most precious possession to run to waste."

ANCIENT WISDOM

Pythagoras, the founding father of geometry, taught that there was a direct connection between semen and the brain. He cautioned that the loss of semen weakens the brain, while its conservation serves to nourish it. This idea was also very prominent in ancient Indian society among the *rishis*. Pythagoras lived a century-long life and such longevity was common among generations of people who adhered to the Pythagorean doctrine. The *rishis* and yogis of India's spiritual culture developed extraordinary mental powers and lived long and healthy lives.

In *Taoist Secrets of Love*, contemporary Taoist teacher Mantak Chia writes, "Because a single drop of semen houses such prodigious life energies, frequent loss of fluid depletes the body systems of their most precious nutrients and speeds the inevitable physical decline into old age. Retaining the seed within the body is the first step in reversing this cycle." About brain nourishment, Omraam Mikhael Aivanhov writes in his *Sexual Force of the Winged Dragon*, "Men and women must use this [sexual] tension to feed and water the cells of their brains."

Lecithin, an organic phosphorized fat, which is the chief constituent of both brain and nerve tissue, is an essential component of semen. The semen consists of a highly concentrated form of blood—the cream of the milk of blood. Besides containing lecithin, semen is rich in calcium, phosphorous, iron, vitamin E, and hormones. With the loss of semen comes the loss of lecithin from the blood and brain when new semen needs to be produced. Conservation of semen through continence leads naturally to increased brain nutrition and increased intellectual energy.

Monastic spiritual culture often involves years of study of philosophy, which requires nourishing the pituitary and pineal glands. The pineal gland is richer in lecithin than any other part of the body. Continence preserves lecithin, which

THE CASE FOR CONTINENCE

is then used by the body to nourish the pineal glands. Thus it is understandable why religious orders often recommend continence for those who wish to live a life of spiritual practice.

Scientific studies on senility conducted a century past by the father of endocrinology, Dr. Brown-Sequard, lend support to the theories of the *rishis* who maintained that retaining vital fluids increases longevity and improves overall health. Professor Brown-Sequard was a prominent physiologist well known for his research work at Harvard. His interest in senility found him engaged in various experiments. These experiments showed a connection between senility and a deficiency of internal secretions from the reproductive glands. Excessive sexual activity can greatly diminish the supply of sperm, which otherwise would be internally secreted. The internal secretions are reabsorbed into the blood and, after passing through the bloodstream, accumulate chiefly in the tissue of the central nervous system. This in turn nourishes the brain. These secretions seem to have a selective affinity for the tissue of the central nervous system based on their similarity in chemical composition, both being rich in phosphates and lecithin. Indeed, no two constituents of the body are so remarkably similar in composition than the sperm and tissue of the central nervous system.

Although he did not discover the cure for senility, which results from the autointoxication of the entire endocrine system and not merely the gonads, Brown-Sequard's work is important and relevant to our discussion. His experiments, in which he found that hormonal injections prepared from the tissue of animals had amazing regenerative effects, serve to substantiate the theories of wise men of the past: that the sexual fluid, the source of regeneration, can if retained increase vitality, including mental powers. His conclusions were verified much later by several research doctors, one of whom, Dr. K. S. Guthrie, in his work *Re-*

ANCIENT WISDOM

generation remarked: "But if the human sperma is as good if not better [than animals], why should not each man preserve his own, instead of wasting this and then procuring other by repulsive and brutal means? . . . Should man inject into himself the testicular secretions of animals when he could preserve his own and keep his body continually at the highest point of vitality?"

Optimum health, increased mental and intellectual power, a solution to overpopulation and venereal disease, and instilling humanity with an increased sense of reverence for the process of creation are all compelling reasons for moving in the direction of a continent lifestyle. But most compelling is the way in which continence assists in the development of spiritual consciousness. To find the spiritual source of our sexual energy will be the most we can do for ourselves and our planet.

The mystics of both East and West have been practitioners of continence for centuries. The East, however, has provided us with more information as to how the sexual energy when controlled and transformed can produce mystical experience.

The Eastern idea of continence is known as *brahmacharya*. It is mandatory for student life within the *ashrama* (living place of the guru). Those who leave student life for marriage on the advice of their guide also live a continent life, engaging in sex only for procreation rather than sensual pleasure. Those who forego marriage throughout life accept the renounced order of *sannyasa* on completing their student life, as do those in married life after their children leave home. It is generally in the renounced order, after many years of spiritual practice, that the heightened effects of continent life begin to show themselves as the fruits of dedication in the form of *brahma-tejas*, spiritual power.

Uninformed persons are more or less controlled by their sexual energy and thus they remain within the world

THE CASE FOR CONTINENCE

of sensual experience. Others by controlling the same gross sexual energy can, at will, produce good progeny and keep optimum health and sound mind. The *sannyasin*, however, masters the sexual energy at the subtle level. *Sannyasis* are also thereby free from the subtle forms of worldly sexual involvement such as the desires for distinction, adoration, and profit. They are free from these desires because they are self-satisfied due to experiencing their higher nature. The real *sannyasis* transform the coal of sexual sensuality into the diamond of self-realization. They live in the world, but are not of it. They have no greed, lust, or envy, which are all painful conditions that inhibit us from giving fully of ourselves to others.

Ojas is the subtle form of sexual energy. Stuart Sovatsky, author of *Tantric Celibacy*, describes *ojas* as "a powerful alchemical distillate of the hormones of sexual motivation." It develops in the body as sexual energy is sublimated during a month-long bodily process. Food is transformed into blood and blood into bodily tissue, bodily tissue is then transformed into mental energy, or *ojas*. If sexual orgasm is indulged in more than once in thirty days, this bodily cycle is thrown off. Thus overharvesting of sexual fluid through frequent orgasm depletes *ojas*, while continence and meditation increase its supply. This energy creates a subtle force (*virya*) that enables one to work in wonderful ways sometimes unseen by the physical eye. The much higher spiritual experience of love of God involves tracing out the infinitely more subtle source of *ojas*. This is done through the culture of a willingness to be again controlled, this time by the source of conscious energy in a divine life, rather than by the material expression of sexual energy as we are in material life. This is an exercise of the inner heart, the transformation of lust into love and the death of the material ego. To come under the influence of the divine energy is to become forever free from the constraints of material illusion. It is the antithesis of illusory life in which we are *used by* the gross sexual energy as slaves of matter, while all the time thinking ourselves the master.

Although it is true that we are masters, it is more as caretakers. The "power" that we derive from dominating matter for our sensual titillation is illusory. It is better to be in harmony with the powers that be. We must rise above the false sense of power and proprietorship derived from material identification and sensuality to understand our proper connection with divinity.

There is much at stake in human life and it is important that we use our valuable human energy for the optimum result. Ultimately we are pleasure seekers by nature. There is pleasure in continence. The pleasure derived from using our sexual energy conscientiously for higher achievement does not involve taking from others under the guise of giving. Anyone who seriously considers the case for continence lays a foundation for ultimate happiness.

Human life is for more than sophisticated animality. We are the caretakers of our planet and its creatures. It is time we develop the courage to do this work, God's work, and bring love and life to all creation. Seeing ourselves as part of an organic whole, we must adopt the thinking of, "What is in it for the whole?" and give up thinking, "What is in it for me?" The personal sacrifice involved in our evolution toward wholeness may seem very great, but it in no way can compare to the greatness of achieving the goal. The virtues of a continent lifestyle have been heralded for ages by some of the world's greatest men and women—the kind our present world needs more of.

LIFE IN THE WOMB

BABIES ARE STILL ONE OF THE MOST desirable commodities, even in today's fast-paced society where sometimes family values take a backseat to professional achievement. In America approximately eight babies are born every minute. Yet it still takes three-quarters of a year to produce each individual tot.

So far, baby making is one commodity that has withstood our passion for mass production. Although we know a lot about babies, the nine or ten months of their fetal development remains in a cloud of mystery and controversy. Thus the questions, "When does life in the womb actually begin?" and "What is the nature of the embryonic experience?" remain unanswered.

Of course many "answers" have been offered. Perhaps the loudest voice heralds from the laboratories of scientific materialism. Since the days of the controlled experiment, the scientific community, characterized as those who "objectively" observe the controlled microcosm and thus "conclusively" understand the macrocosm, has enjoyed a great deal of credibility. Such scientific men and women are in search of the *material conditions* that give rise to life as we know it. As such they have offered various theories regarding life in the womb, all of which remain just that—theories—mostly dehumanizing ones.

Popular religion, another loud voice in history, has for the most part "believed" in one thing but failed to explain it rationally. The "religious" believe that life begins at the time of conception, but for them life in general is an inexplicable miracle, the "breath of God." The general populace seems to schizophrenically side with the religious sentiment but operate under a scientifically governed worldview.

ANCIENT WISDOM

Considerably hidden in all of this is the view of the mystics. Mysticism has been described as the search for the one spiritual reality, which lies beyond the rituals of the world's many religions. Although it has a presence in every religious tradition, its constituency is always rather small in comparison to the popularized versions of any particular tradition, and it is often unpopular within the tradition itself. But mystics have definitively answered these questions concerning life's origin and life in the womb—rationally, yet spiritually—long ago. There is good reason to suspect that their answers are more accurate than the scientific or religious views, inasmuch as the mystics actually live within the conceptions they advocate. Their lives are not a bluff. Their faith is not a mere belief or sophisticated theory but an experience and realization that translates into practical action.

Generally speaking, according to the mystics, material conditions do not give rise to life at all; rather, life—consciousness—gives rise to material conditions, and thus life exists already, everywhere and at all times. Nobel laureate and biologist George Wald, in his quest to understand the nature of life, has confessed to being somewhat bewildered as to how accommodating our universe is to life, when scientifically speaking it is supposed to be a fluke, an accident. Later, when he came in touch with Eastern mysticism, he concluded that he had found the missing link: the universe is so accommodating to life because consciousness has been here all along. Thus the question, "When does life within the womb begin?" is answered much differently and with a louder ring of certainty by those who embrace the perennial philosophy of the mystic traditions. Moreover, the mystics' answer regarding the nature of life within the womb affords insights yet to be considered in prenatal psychology. Let's consider the mystic's view on life in the womb in light of recent technological developments.

Communication with the fetus has become popular, although all attempts to date are primitive at best. The recently invented "pregaphone," a device intended to make fetal communications more feasible, is a good example. The use of the pregaphone, which is said to allow the parents the chance to make "noises" that their child-to-be can hear and to hear sounds uttered from within the womb, implies that the development of the consciousness of the fetus is only very slight, less than that of the newly born. Thus in this conception there is not much we can say to the unborn even if we improve the technology for communication.

In his famous book, *The Secret Life of the Unborn Child*, Dr. Thomas Verny offers considerable evidence that the fetus has the subtle ability to perceive the goings-on outside of the womb. Still, according to Verny, the fetus is only in the primal stage of conscious development. Yet some of his own evidence for consciousness within the womb suggests another scenario. He cites the example of Boris Brott, conductor of the Hamilton (Ontario) Philharmonic Symphony, who learned the cello lines to certain scores within the womb. What appeared to Brott as his mystic ability of precognition of cello lines in scores he conducted for the first time was later demystified when he found that his mother, a cello enthusiast, had regularly played those lines during her pregnancy. But certainly learning the cello requires considerably more awareness than that of a newborn child. Thus as many mystics contend, perhaps the state of consciousness within the womb is greater than commonly considered.

Prenatal psychology has in recent years gained credibility in the scientific community due to the appearance of consistent data in support of consciousness within the womb. Such studies have offered a strong challenge to the Freudian theory that personality develops only after the second

ANCIENT WISDOM

year following birth. While it may be true that the fetus' material personality begins its formation within the womb, many mystics teach that its *spiritual* development generally decreases as the material or karmic personality takes hold. According to some traditions, the traumatic experience of birth altogether suppresses spiritual consciousness. It then continues to be stifled by the ego-enforcing treatment of spiritually underdeveloped parents. Most infants are encouraged to think that they are indeed the center of life itself by those parents similarly ego-absorbed, who see their child as the extension of their own material "selfhood."

Could it be then that the unborn have something to teach us? Is there a point at which the unborn experience heightened spiritual consciousness? Experiments of Igor Charkrovosky, a Russian biologist and pioneer in "water birthing" documented in Erik Sidenbladh's book *Water Babies*, strongly suggest that easing the trauma of birth heightens the potential for the development of paranormal psychic abilities. Charkrovosky believes that the delicate, finer brain functions that are necessary for such abilities are destroyed during traumatic births. Thus it *is* possible that such abilities and heightened spiritual consciousness are present within the womb, only to be lost at birth. In this conception, the transition from one birth to the next offers a time of reflection on the purpose of our existence. However, as we approach the door to the outside world, the force of our *karma* takes hold and our spiritual sense is lost. It can be regained permanently only through its voluntary culture in our post-birth material life—not an easy task, given the present condition of our society.

This flicker of light in the darkness of our material sojourn has been described in several ancient Sanskrit texts. The *Bhagavat Purana*, for example, offers a graphic account of life in the womb. But we must preface this

LIFE IN THE WOMB

account by first reflecting on the value of such literature.

Such texts are not to be dismissed as old religious books. The term *religion*—in which you have yours and I have mine—is a modern development. In previous times, when these Sanskrit texts were written, the authors were engaged not in "their" religion but rather in an investigation into the very nature of being, which in their experience included psychic and spiritual dimensions. These mystics were not mere Sunday churchgoers nor were they scientists employed in pursuit of knowledge in government laboratories. They were spiritual scientists of overwhelming integrity, who did not allow themselves to be implicated in the contradictory roles of peace-searching and weapon-making in order to make ends meet. Thus their accounts of the nature of life and its purpose are at least worthy of our unbiased consideration.

Regarding life in the womb the mystics have not painted a very pretty picture. Much of the discussion parallels what we know from modern science. But there are three major differences. The first is how consciousness enters the sperm, thus making possible the fruitful combination of sperm and ovum and the development of a particular karmic body.

The second is that the overall emphasis is different: the philosophical ramifications of what takes place are brought out, rather than a mere mechanical description. The abominable conditions which the fetus is forced to tolerate (wherein along with the fetus' own development, worms are also born of his/her mother's womb out of fermentation, who in turn feed off their "brother/sister's" fetus body) are discussed in such a way as to cause one to seriously consider the peril of birth. Ordinarily birth is seen in a positive light as a beautiful experience. It is one, however, that nearly every mother during labor swears she will never submit to again. Similarly, any sane adult upon reading the descriptions of life in the womb recorded in such texts will also conclude that taking birth is as much or more painful than giving birth.

Although life in the womb, as described in the *Bhagavat*, is so painful that the living being is forced into near unconsciousness, during the last months a change occurs. This is the third difference from the surface analysis of "Dr. Science." After the seventh month of pregnancy, as the unborn with face down approaches the doorway to life, scores of past lives' experiences pass through the fetus' mind like a serial, reminding the fetus of the tribulations of *many* births and deaths, diseases and old age. The general purpose of life—to transcend this endless cycle and enter into God consciousness—comes to the forefront of embryonic consciousness. And what does the living being do? Here again a different theme emerges: the living being prays not to have to take birth! How bad can life be?!

It may not be that bad, relatively speaking. In comparison to the previous description of the conditions within the womb it would be safe to say that it is pretty good. The point of this narration, however, is that the living being has the opportunity, at least momentarily, to consider our world and material life from a different perspective, one in which the absolutes of life take precedence. We have all heard that when we leave this world we cannot take anything with us; time and tide wait for no man. These are absolutes for all people. They are laws of nature.

The idea of living for something that will end without warning is somewhat unappealing. It is said in the *Vedas* that intelligence that is qualitatively comprised of the material mode of goodness, as opposed to the influences of passion and ignorance, is characterized by the inability to tolerate the idea of having to live in a world that has no endurance. Such intelligence propels us into a life of value-seeking. Qualitatively passionate intelligence, on the other hand, forces the mind and senses to create all kinds of conveniences, many of which in the name of *our* comfort bring about discomfort for others, and in the long run even for ourselves. And intelligence influenced by the material mode of ignorance directs us towards intoxication, madness, and sleep. This combination of passion and ignorance makes us, at best, busy for the wrong reasons. It makes us busy for the acquisition of "things" rather than for a life of higher values. I think it's safe to say we are experiencing this now, and these "old religious books" have delineated how this comes about by scrutinizing material nature and dividing it into three *modus operandi*. If intelligence in material goodness puts our head on straight for a life in which the spiritual comes first, and this life is seen as a progression to a higher life rather than a finality, just imagine then a moment of pure *spiritual* consciousness—an infinitely more profound moment than hundreds of lives of ordinary material experience.

The idea is that when this profound experience occurs it enables us to tolerate life within the womb; otherwise, the situation being intolerable, we would be rendered practically unconscious. And because the ordinary material sense experience after birth is one that reinforces the illusion of bodily identification—black, white, Asian, American, man, woman, and so on—one who recognizes that for even a moment prays to avoid such an entangling network of self-deception, which only leads one in a circle back into another womb.

In an extraordinary case, the ancient sage Shukadeva Goswami, the principal speaker in the *Bhagavat Purana*, is said to have held on to this consciousness and by its force remained within the womb for sixteen years. He took birth only after gaining divine assurance that his life would be free of family encumbrances in order that he might have the leisure to further pursue a transcendental life. Whether this narration is fact or mere legend, in either case it affords a great lesson. However wonderful our ordinary life may seem on the surface, if it proves to be an impediment to our ultimate progress as an evolving soul, it should be reevaluated. Such thinking in fact can transform our "ordinary" life into one of profound meaning, thus steering us in the direction of the supernal.

Obviously, most people have a different experience from that of Shukadeva. If they have moments of pure consciousness within the womb, they cannot remain with those moments, but submit to the force of their *karma* and undergo the trauma of birth, thus forgetting everything, even the previous life within the womb. As they develop in material consciousness, they often drift so far from reality as to advocate that there is little if any life within the womb. In this way scientific materialism, the result of the trauma of birth and a lifetime of misplaced values, leaves humanity bewildered, wondering about life.

Here a vote for less traumatic births is in order for starters. But there is more to it than that. Let us find the hidden beauty of birth, life, and even death. That beauty can be realized by those who conscientiously pursue spiritual values and not merely religious rituals. This kind of life is one in which substance prevails over form, as it rightfully should. If birth becomes the opportunity to pursue the glimpse of pure consciousness experienced in the womb, then life becomes the opportunity to transcend death. In this context so-called death becomes a welcome sight and fear is altogether vanquished.

As we near the twenty-first century, human society with all of its scientific advancement needs to change its direction. The time has come to make birth a desirable and truly beautiful experience by making life what it should be—communion with the divine, free from religious dogma and scientific materialism.

MAKING SENSE WITH SCENTS

COSMETICS AND FRAGRANCES have been used in human society since time immemorial. Those of ancient times who drew upon nature's resources, extracting essential oils and other natural ingredients, probably never thought that it would become a multibillion dollar enterprise.

Neither could they have conceived of the extent to which industrially produced fragrances and cosmetics would in the future serve to degrade society. The unfortunate fact is that the primary characteristic of the exploitative culture in which we live is that it invariably lends to the degradation and adulteration of even the most noble practices.

Today, Americans spend $1.5 billion annually on facial cosmetics, lotions, and potions. One congressional study puts the amount Americans spend on trying to turn back the clock at closer to $3 billion yearly. And consumer reports have listed the overall U.S. expenditure on cosmetics including toiletries at $24.2 billion for 1986 alone.

Besides the high cost, today's fragrance and cosmetic industry has great potential for doing harm. Because the FDA does not have enough authority to effectively regulate cosmetics, products which may be hazardous are marketed. About 125 ingredients available for use in cosmetics are suspected carcinogens, and about twenty-five are suspected of causing birth defects. Another thirty ingredients are known to cause cancer, although the precise extent of their ability to cause cancer through cosmetic use has not been determined. According to a report published by the U.S. General Accounting Office in August of 1978 and reprinted in *Being Beautiful*, "Manufacturers do not have to determine the safety of their products before selling them or tell the

ANCIENT WISDOM

FDA what products they are selling and what ingredients are used in them. . . . As a result, hazardous cosmetics can be marketed until the FDA obtains information to prove that the product may be injurious to users."

Fragrance ingredients are highest on the list of cosmetic products that cause allergic reactions. According to *FDA Consumer* (May 1987) a New Jersey cosmetic manufacturer recalled a brand of eye makeup that could cause serious harm to or even blindness in its users. One must also keep in mind that cosmetic lotions, hair dyes, and perfumes do not remain on the surface of the skin—they soak in. Hair dye is a good example. According to *Consumer Reports* magazine (August 1979), coal-tar chemicals used in hair dyes, which are known to cause mutations, readily penetrate the scalp and enter the blood stream. Thus all parts of the body, including a developing fetus in a pregnant mother, risk exposure. In addition, mutations in the immature eggs of a woman's ovaries could be transmitted to future generations.

Things have changed quite a bit over the years. Originally, fragrances derived from essential oils were used in religious rituals, and they were used therapeutically in medical treatment, both mental and physical, as well as for beauty care. So cosmetics used to enhance natural beauty were simultaneously agents for improved health. Egyptian high priests who served as medical practitioners developed many beauty treatments to alleviate or cure afflictions of the skin or scalp. Most significant among these were the oils and unguents originally intended to preserve the dead, which came to be used to smooth or rejuvenate living skin. This partnership of cosmetics and medicine lasted well into the Middle Ages.

The Indian eye shadow *kardil* is another example. *Kardil,* while giving the eye a beautiful, elongated appear-

MAKING SENSE WITH SCENTS

ance (from which the term "lotus eyes" comes), actually improves vision. Other cosmetic markings in Indian society act as social indications, such as the *bindi*, a red dot in the middle of the forehead, that a woman wears to indicate that she is married. In ancient India, the body was considered a temple of God. Thus devotees of various persuasions decorated their foreheads with a clay "makeup" known as *tilak*, which externally distinguished one religious sect from another. Essential oils and their derivative—incense—were used in temple worship. The Deities in the temples were massaged daily with scented oil, and flavored oil extracts were used in preparing drinks to offer to them.

In the Jewish tradition, we also find that aromatics were used regularly in religious rituals. In Exodus 30:22-31, one of the commandments given by God to Moses was to make holy oils and incense. The oil was used for the anointing of rabbis and was not for common use; the incense was intended exclusively for religious ceremonies.

Centuries ago, the Chinese, Tibetans, Egyptians, Babylonians, Persians, Greeks, Romans, Aztecs, and Hindus all used essential oils therapeutically, and it was in ancient Hindu society that aromatherapy emerged as a branch of the life-science known as ayurveda. Ayurveda is perhaps the only science of ancient medicine that has remained alive since the time of its first appearance in human society, which was about five thousand years ago.

Ancient Hindus vaporized floral and herbal oils in small pots of boiling water to soften the skin, soothe the mind, and normalize the functions of various glands. The annals of ayurvedic medicine even specify which oils are used for which glands. The Aztecs also vaporized oils. They had vapor rooms called *temezcalls* in which hot, dry air was filled with the vapors of flower and herb oils rising from a small pool of hot stones and water. These vapors were used

ANCIENT WISDOM

to stimulate circulation, soften the skin, and contribute to a relaxed state of mind. And the famous Roman baths always contained a special perfume room called an *unctuarium*, where the body was massaged with perfumed oils following the bath.

In the times when aromatics were the *materia medica*, though the scents may have been enjoyable, that was purely incidental. It was not until the 1700s that aromatics came to be used mainly for sensual enjoyment. Nowadays, fragrances and cosmetics are for the most part identified with beauty enhancement, and a great many of them are not comprised of natural ingredients or essential oils. Apparently, in many minds the idea that the soul within is the real beauty of life has been upstaged by the idea that beauty depends on a layer of synthetic poisons and pollutants. Artificial concoctions to beautify the body are in fact poisonous to the user and injurious to other living beings in the course of their production—such as in the case of animal experimentation—and are a rather ugly reminder of the confused, self-centered sense of purpose with which many of us choose to live.

The declining use of aromatics as medicine coincided with two other historical developments. One was the "golden age" in the art of perfumery, which began in the eighteenth century when the region surrounding the town of Grasse in the south of France became a center for the growing of aromatic plants and the extraction of essences for use in perfumes. This brought the use of aromatics for purposes of enjoyment to levels that had never been possible before by greatly increasing the quantity and upgrading the quality of the essences that are used in creating the blended compositions that today we call perfume.

At the same time, the development of synthetic drug therapies for the treatment of disease provided an alternative to the botanical methods that had predominated up to that time. Once the power of drugs was recognized, most research efforts were turned in that direction. Botanicals ceased to be of interest except as starting materials from which isolated chemicals could be extracted.

In the East, however, especially in India and China, the traditional ways did not fall into disuse as they did in Western society. When modern medicine reached Asia, it did not replace botanical medicine but existed side by side with it. Among peasant cultures in Europe, which cannot afford modern doctors, drugs, and hospitals, the botanical lore of antiquity has been preserved and actively practiced. It is to these cultures that modern researchers of aromatherapy turn to for answers to satisfy their inquires.

Most aromatherapists today credit India and France with being their two greatest sources of knowledge and inspiration. The term *aromatherapy* was coined during World War I by a Frenchman named Rene Maurice Gattefosse, publisher of *La Parfumerie Moderne,* and a manufacturer-chemist-perfumer who had long been interested in the hygienic and antiseptic properties of essential oils. During the war he was assigned to a frontline hospital receiving station for seriously injured soldiers. There he used essential oils in the treatment of burns and flesh wounds and is reported to have prevented gangrene, healed burns, and helped develop scar tissue in mutilated limbs through therapy with aromatics. Later he started a factory for producing aromatic materials and a pharmaceutical firm to promote the use of medical discoveries made in his research laboratories.

One of his more well-known followers, Austrian-born biochemist Marguerite Maury, opened a clinic in London in the '60s, and those inspired by her brought the science to the Americas. According to Maury, "Of the greatest

ANCIENT WISDOM

interest is the effect of fragrances on the psychic and mental state of the individual. The power of perception becomes clearer and more acute and there is a feeling of having, to a certain extent, outstripped events. . . . It might even be said that the emotional trouble which in general obscures our perception is practically suppressed."

The sense of smell operates to a large extent on the subconscious level. The olfactory nerves are directly connected to the most primitive part of our brain, the limbic system, which regulates sensory motor activities. It is also connected with the sexual urge and behavioral mechanisms. When the olfactory bulb is stimulated, it sends electrical signals to the limbic system, and as a result one's emotional behavior is affected. Interestingly, the French verb *sentir* — "to smell"—also means "to feel."

Our olfactory nerves are also closely related to our memory. French psychoanalyst Andre Virel used fragrances to bring out hidden memories, and scents are often used to revive one's memory in the way of bringing one back to consciousness after fainting. The sense of smell also affects our ability to taste. While suffering from a cold, for example, we cannot fully taste the foods we eat. Overall, bringing our sense of smell in connection with the right aroma can dramatically influence our health and mental stability, and even help to create an atmosphere conducive to higher spiritual thought.

Modern-day aromatherapists may use over four hundred essential oils. These oils are extracted from various parts of the plants in which they are found: roots, leaves, resins, flowers, seeds, bark, or the rinds of fruit. They are extracted by steam or water distillation. After cooling the distillate, the non-water soluble essential oil separates from the water. In many cases minute, water-soluble fractions remain dissolved in the water and may be used in that form.

MAKING SENSE WITH SCENTS

Because this is not a highly technical procedure, it has the potential to develop more as a cottage industry in the future, thereby providing a less expensive and more wholesome alternative to the present-day mass production of synthetic fragrances.

Many of the eight hundred botanical species that yield essential oil are today rarely used in the fragrance industry and are therefore unavailable commercially. Thus it is vital that new sources for these oils be developed. Today much of the research and development work in essential oils is being conducted in India at the Dehra Dun Research Institute and many of the rare oils are produced only in India. Until the production of these essential oils in reestablished on a wider scale, they remain an endangered species.

Most therapists agree on the use of particular scents for specific ailments. At the same time there is some room for variation inasmuch as people may react differently to aromas. This is not as much the case in dealing with specific physical diseases, which is more exacting, as it is when dealing with the conditions of the mind. According to Robert B. Tisserand, author of *The Art of Aromatherapy*, "Each essence has its own personality, its own set of attributes, and this can be used to bring out certain qualities in us; helping us to see ourselves more clearly, to understand our faults, and to let the beauty and joy of our souls breathe a fresh, summery fragrance through our minds."

Modern Western society would do well to take a second look at its painted faces, and take a second whiff of the scents of its "natives" who are largely engaged in little more than an extended form of the mating ritual. The use of fragrances and cosmetics beyond mere beauty enhancement is a concept that is gaining ground in society today, as is the production of more natural and healthy cosmetics in

ANCIENT WISDOM

general. As it becomes more popular, we will undoubtedly find that millions of dollars can then be used for worthier causes, and if we revive the original use of essential oils as an aid to spiritual practices, then perhaps we will also find human society moving more within the embrace of the divine.

AYURVEDA OR ALLOPATHY?

INDIA SUFFERS TODAY MORE through the world's ignorance of her achievements than from the absence of achievements. Medicine is a prime example. The ancient medical science of ayurveda, which is experiencing a partial renaissance at present, is perhaps the most sophisticated and comprehensive approach to health care the world has ever known.

A comparison of ayurveda and allopathy reveals serious problems with the allopathic approach. Although modern medicine is thought to have replaced superstition and folk medicine, in comparison to the original ayurvedic science, allopathy could be viewed as but an extension of the guesswork and superstition it is thought to have replaced—a mere poking in the dark at the expense of our planet and its life forms.

Why and how has such a great science as ayurveda been practically lost? The answer lies principally in foreign domination. Foreign domination lasted in India for over one thousand years, beginning with the Moghul tribes and ending with the British Raj. At least it has formally ended with the British; India has yet to reconstruct its great history, and in the meantime it continues to suffer from subtle foreign academic domination. While India attempts to piece together the scraps of paper shredded by its foreign rulers, India's academicians continue to be heavily influenced by a primarily Eurocentric view of cultural and scientific evolution.

Ironically, both foreign domination and the allopathic approach to medicine arise from the same mentality of self-assertion. The present-day revival of ayurveda can also be

ANCIENT WISDOM

understood to be the result of the conscious mind behind it—"The meek shall inherit the earth." The current upsurge of interest in ayurveda is not as much an interest in India and her history as it is a groping for meaning in a world dominated by atomism, which has left many unfulfilled at present and even terrified about our future. When we speak of ayurveda, we speak of a well thought-out worldview, which if put into practice can do much to remedy our modern-day maladies—biological, psychological, social, environmental, and spiritual. A comparison of the methodologies, conceptual framework, origins, and disease causation theories of ayurveda and allopathy will prove this.

METHODOLOGIES

The ancient *rishis* (enlightened sages) of India employed a scientific methodology that allowed them to understand the mysteries of life, both spiritual and material. In addition to providing them with thorough knowledge of the life processes, their methodology provided the basis to analyze and determine the medicinal value of plants, minerals, and animals—long before the invention of microscopes, analytical chemistry, and other tools of the Western scientific method.

In comparison to ayurveda's comprehensive approach to acquiring knowledge, the Western scientific method is clearly inferior. The Western approach to acquiring knowledge is based upon three steps: 1) hypothesis, 2) experimentation and observation, and 3) theory or conclusion. Vedic science, on the other hand, uses three proofs, or *pramana*, two of which entirely cover the ground encompassed by the Western scientific method. This leaves a third type of evidence at the disposal of the Vedic scientists, giving them a decisive edge over their Western counterparts. As we shall see, this third means of acquiring knowledge takes us to the heart of the difference between these two approaches.

AYURVEDA OR ALLOPATHY?

The first limb of the Vedic means for arriving at truth is *pratyaksha*, or direct sense perception, including the observations of others. The second is *anuman*, or logical inference. The last and most important limb is *shabda pramana*, or hearing from authoritative sources, such as realized souls, for whom there is an observable criteria, and revealed scriptures, which are the writings of previous saints.

CONCEPTUAL FRAMEWORK AND BASIC CONCEPTS

Ayurvedic science's premise is that the health of the soul is primary, and everything else revolves around that ultimate state of well-being. Ayurveda has a clear conception of consciousness, intellect, mind, and body, understanding them to be distinct hierarchical realities that evolve from the supreme consciousness to individual consciousness on down. Thus ayurveda is well-equipped to care for all states of disease. Physical, mental, emotional, social, and environmental diseases are all within its scope.

On the level of physical health, which is the primary if not exclusive concern of allopathy, ayurvedic scientists were at least as competent as modern allopaths in dealing with any ailment, including surgical operations, which were done under herbal anesthetic. Surgical procedures in ayurveda are recorded in the *Shushruta Samhita* (1000 B.C.E.). Any number of modern-day operations, from routine appendectomies to complex organ transplants are mentioned therein. These, however, were not the pride of ayurveda. They were last resort measures that were necessary only a fraction of the time in comparison to our modern medical system. This was so because of ayurveda's ability to cure ailments without surgery and ayurveda's worldview, which holds nonviolence as an esteemed virtue to be cultivated by all.

The Vedic *rishis* divided sentient beings into two broad categories: "moving," such as humans, animals, birds,

ANCIENT WISDOM

aquatics; and "non-moving," such as plants. This prevented such misconceptions as Descart's miscalculation that animals were little more than machines. The *rishis* understood the nature of consciousness and biological life processes in such a thorough way that not only could most substances produced by the animal, mineral, and plant kingdom be used to compose medicine, but branches of ayurveda were developed that treated disease in animals and plants. The sensitivity of the *rishis* was such that they discouraged not only the exploitation of the animal kingdom, but the exploitation of the plant and mineral kingdoms as well, thus preventing the type of environmental crisis that Western science has brought upon us.

The basic psychosomatic constitutions, or *doshadhatus,* delineated in ayurveda as *vata, pitta,* and *kapha,* provide the overall conceptual framework on which to build a complete understanding of the living world. The *doshadhatus* are: 1) *vatta,* the bodily airs; 2) *pitta,* the bodily fires; and 3) *kapha,* the bodily fluids. These were translated into English long ago as wind, bile, and mucous. These three psychosomatic constitutions are present in every living being. Health is said to be a perfect balance of all three.

The *tridosha* are the basic building blocks of life, and they make up a hierarchy called *saptadhatu*: 1) food nutrients, 2) blood, 3) flesh, 4) fat and connecting tissues, 5) bone, 6) bone marrow and cerebrospinal fluid, and 7) semen or ovum. Besides *doshadhatu* and *saptadhatu,* ayurveda describes a third *dhatu: rasadhatu,* the system of *rasas,* or tastes. The *rasas,* which are six in number, are derived from foods and the environment. They nourish the bodily tissues in different ways and form the basis for ayurvedic dietetics and herbology. These three systems—*doshadhatu, saptadhatu,* and *rasadhatu*—are foundational to all ayurvedic understanding. The *tridosha* framework, which determines the

AYURVEDA OR ALLOPATHY?

individual constitution of every person, causes the medical practitioner to not only deal with every patient as a unique individual, but every disease as a unique disturbance.

All these systems are understood within the conception of the *triguna*, which views the phenomenal world in terms of its three principal modes of influence: *sattva* (clarity), *rajas* (passion), and *tamas* (darkness). These trimodal influences, the five gross elements (ether [space], air, fire, water, and earth), and the subtle elements of mind, intellect, and material ego constitute our biological and psychic bodies and the entire world of material experience. If there is any conceptual framework in allopathy from which its successes arise, it is the simplistic idea that all life is reducible to biochemical and ultimately molecular processes. Ayurveda, however, accepts a hierarchical structure of realities culminating in the divine. Although allopathy's view is well-formed, it has come about as a result of experimentation; therefore, it does not rest on a secure foundation, but formulates concepts based on conjecture derived from ongoing experimentation. While ayurveda works from a broad base down to specifics, allopathy collects data from the world and then tries to draw conclusions about the nature of truth—a clearly speculative and inferior approach.

The problem with the modern scientific approach is twofold: one, a view based solely on experimentally derived data is subject to change when new and even contradictory data arises through subsequent experimentation. This unstable structure can totter at any time, and thus it would be difficult to build a stable society upon it. For example, entire schools of medical education and funding for medical projects would be risky ventures, because everything could change if conflicting verifiable data arises. Although it seems laudable theoretically to experiment, go forward, and be prepared to change direction at any time, it is highly impractical on a societal level. This brings us to the second problem, which is that consistent data does arise regularly, challenging the existing paradigm. But due to the fact that there is so much at stake, it is often ignored, or experimentation loses its objectivity inasmuch as it produces only data that conforms with the existing worldview. In other words, speculation, which modern medicine is seeded in, invariably lends to loss of integrity. Ironically, it is often billed as the noble pursuit of truth.

Experimentation is undoubtedly a valid means of acquiring relative knowledge, but it must be conducted within a larger framework that includes descending knowledge in order that it not degenerate into self-deception. Experimentation conducted within ayurveda either rejects or accepts evidence based on whether it is or is not contradictory to descending knowledge, the spiritual worldview.

ORIGINS

The knowledge of ayurveda is of a divine origin, whereas allopathy is arrived at though experimental prodding of matter. Although experimentation is an important part of *pramana*, in ayurveda it is carried on within a larger conceptual framework based on descending knowledge. Again, Western medicine lacks guidance from higher intelligence. Ayurveda descends from higher intelligence and thus is not a product of conditioned human reasoning, which is full of faults. The allopathic approach is much more akin to the medicine of uncivilized peoples than ayurveda is, although modern medicine men would have it seem otherwise. Here the unbiased will have to ask themselves, "Is there perfect knowledge?" If the answer is "no," then we may as well stop there. But Western thinking assumes that there is perfect knowledge to which we can evolve. However, the questionable means of evolution involves utilizing imperfect instruments and human frailties.

AYURVEDA OR ALLOPATHY?

Vedic science also admits to perfect knowledge, but being that it is perfect, that knowledge is considered superior to humanity, and thus human society can attain it only if it chooses to reveal itself. Although the knowledge of ayurveda is basically secular, dealing with the phenomenal world, ayurveda believes that the material world is a reflection of the spiritual plane.

Allopathy's rational methodology, it must be remembered, arose as a reaction to irrational European reliance on incantations and superstition that could be considered a vitiated form of the rational spirituality of ancient India. Allopathy is an overreaction to unscientific medicine and pseudospirituality, neither of which are elements of ayurveda. It sprang not from the spiritual platform, but the speculative mental fabric of "religious" men of the time. Although the founding fathers of the new European era of reason "believed in God," their spiritual premise was so weak that they could not foresee that the new concepts they introduced would develop into the greatest nemesis of their ill-conceived spirituality. Not so for rational Vedic spirituality, however, which even today is having an impact on many of the world's greatest scientific minds, as is its subsidiary, ayurveda.

Ayurveda is wholly different from the neo-Aristotelian paradigm reigning in Europe before the reactionary advent of modern medicine. While modern medicine's votaries sought to secure an experimentally testable method to replace *ad hoc* medicine, ayurvedic *vaidyas* (physicians) were employing their own scientific, experimentally testable methodology and divine insight within the *dhatudosha* framework.

Although modern medicine is credited with successfully treating disease, it may really only have succeeded in causing what is now called chronic disease. Because it arises

ANCIENT WISDOM

as a reaction to ignorance, it is only a half-truth at best. Reactionary solutions are never complete solutions. Many people in the West are attempting to bring about a Hegelian synthesis of ancient Eastern medicine and allopathy. Although I will explore this idea in my conclusion, Eastern medicine is foundationally different from modern medicine, which makes such a synthesis almost impossible. Of the two foundations, conventional medical knowledge in the West rests on an enormous yet flimsy infrastructure of experimental achievements. Thus it lacks the comprehensiveness of true medical wisdom.

DISEASE CAUSATION/CURE

The Eastern and Western approaches to disease causation are fundamentally different from each other and for that matter so is what they consider disease. In the *Charaka Samhita*, an authoritative ayurvedic text, we find the following: "As the age of truth declines, some people find themselves in possession of too much *adana* (greed), which leads to *gaurava* (heaviness in the body and mind). This condition leads to *srama* (lethargy), which leads to *alasya* (laziness). Laziness leads to *sanchaya*, or hoarding, which leads to *parigraha*, or capturing what belongs to others. *Parigraha* leads to further greed and avarice (*lobha*). This chain of demoralized actions continues through treachery, falsehood, uncurbed desires, anger and wrath, vanity, hatred, cruelty, shock, fear, distress, sorrow, and anxiety. Then the bodies and the minds of the people deteriorate and become easy prey to disease. Thus even the span of life is shortened."

Further, the *Charaka Samhita* describes an interesting condition called the epidemic of arms: "When greed, anger, avarice, pride, and vanity hold sway over people's minds, they, despising the weak and irrespective of the victim being their own kith and kin, take to invading and destroying each other." Thus the tie between immoral and improper

AYURVEDA OR ALLOPATHY?

action and disease causation is clearly indicated in ayurveda. The *Charaka Samhita* goes on to describe other causative factors, linking the overall mental, physical, and moral health of the people with the moral integrity of the heads of the family, village, city, state, and nation.

The Western medical system lacks a complete causative theory. Ayurveda's doctrine of *karma* is a well-developed and reasonable concept. Simply put, it extends into the moral realm the atomic notion that each action has an equal and opposite reaction. This doctrine deserves to be distanced with dignity from the popular simplistic understanding of its principles often mentioned by T.V. hosts in jest. This is especially so when biomedicine is now at an impasse on account of its primitive theory of disease causation, a theory that if really thought out could certainly bring a few laughs. Obvious causative influences—such as psychological, social, and environmental—cannot be admitted as such due to the reductionist worldview of allopathy. But can any sane person continue to insist that the mind, the environment, and social circumstances do not directly influence our physiology or, worse still, insist that a hierarchical reality above the physical plane does not exist at all?

According to allopathy, disease is a result of invading organisms, metabolic imbalances, tissue degeneration, and so on. In the model of infectious disease, for example, the invading agent is to be tracked down and killed. This approach is genocidal; it attempts to annihilate entire species of the vast microscopic world. According to ayurveda, disease is an imbalance in the body; there is no question of killing. Free from the folly of attempting to kill everything, ayurveda recognizes the inscrutable will of the Supreme, and the right to life of even the microorganisms. The attack-and-destroy methods of modern medicine are as foreign to the *rishis* of ayurveda as the modern battlefield is to their peaceful hermitages. What is the chance of allopathy achieving its goal of a germ-proof world, anyway? At present, modern science is creating the conditions that give rise to increasingly resistant strains of viruses and bacteria. Thus the greatest causal factor of disease in allopathy may well be itself.

CONCLUSION

At the risk of sharp criticism, I have highlighted several of the shortcomings of modern medicine. But if we consider the treatment of ayurveda by modern medical advocates, it seems justifiable. Yet what the world needs is something more than just revealing the shortcomings of modern medicine, although it is a necessary beginning. Modern medicine has fed the modern world the pill of propaganda to the point of mass addiction. Thus many of us need to be jolted from our firm faith in a system of medicine that is far from perfect. My criticism of allopathy is not the voice of a lone fanatic. There is considerable discontent with modern medicine, not only from the ranks of alternative medicine but from allopathic quarters as well. That modern medicine needs help is no secret to the informed.

The last decade has seen a tremendous interest in alternative medicine, and recently ayurveda in particular is receiving attention. The reasons for this are varied, from the economics of costly research involved in allopathy to the side effects of drugs, which in turn require more drugs *ad infinitum*. The doctor/patient relationship is also at a low ebb in allopathy, and many people are seeking more personal care and participation in cure.

Unknown to many is the fact that modern medicine has paid considerable attention to ayurveda in search of medicinal plants from which to extract new and effective drugs. A number of world agencies have placed their faith in traditional medicine including ayurveda. WHO, UNIDO, and UNESCO all have recognized the importance of me-

AYURVEDA OR ALLOPATHY?

dicinal plants, encouraging research so that herbal medicines can be put to better and more efficient use. Yet almost all of the interest in ayurveda in the allopathic medical community is aimed at finding herbal remedies, and the soul of ayurveda does not rest in herbal formulas. Its value is being determined today in allopathic quarters largely, if not entirely, through the measured effectiveness of its recommended medicinal plants, which allopathy uses in suppressing the symptoms of disease. Little if any consideration is being given to the philosophy of ayurveda. But it is in the investigation of the conceptual framework of ayurveda that hope for an improved medical care system for our modern world lies, not in adding herbal formulas to the edifice of allopathy. If there is to be any merger of allopathy and ayurveda, it can only be one in which the broader foundation of ayurveda is complemented by various experimental findings of allopathy, not vice versa.

It is no longer permissible to ignore the diseased state of our environment, social conditions, and mental states, and continue to extol the virtues of our system of medicine. We need a system of medicine that acknowledges that these are contributing factors to disease. The comprehensive worldview—a spiritual and rational one—of which ayurveda is a part may therefore be worth attempting to resurrect. This is especially so when interest in Eastern medicine and philosophy is surfacing in many Western scientific circles. If one questions just how much of this ancient science can be revived, the answer lies in the fact that it is descending knowledge. It can be revived in proportion to our realization of our utter necessity for higher guidance, lost as we are in a maze of guesswork.

An exhaustive comparison of ayurveda and allopathy is a study well worth undertaking. From its methodology to its conceptual framework, origin, disease causation

ANCIENT WISDOM

theory, and approaches to cure, ayurveda has much to offer. The broader scope of Eastern medicine is hard to deny, and ayurveda is the mother of all Eastern medical disciplines, including Chinese and Tibetan medicine. If it appears to fall short on account of the advances in specialized fields of allopathy, that may in fact be to its credit. Implementation of the worldview of ayurveda could very well diminish the need for many of the "advancements" of allopathy.

Ayurveda is not on the same level as pre-industrial revolution medical developments in Europe, as many would like us to think. Had this been recognized long ago, the development of European medicine, and science in general, could perhaps have avoided the long detour they have taken in the form of modern science and medicine.

VOICE OF TRANSCENDENCE

IF WE SPEND
THE BETTER PORTION OF OUR
LIVES IN PURSUIT OF THE TRUTH,
CERTAINLY THE TRUTH
WILL PRESENT ITSELF BEFORE US.
AT THAT TIME, HOWEVER,
WE WILL HAVE TO ASK
OURSELVES IF IT IS THE TRUTH
WE WANTED AFTER ALL.

THE HEART OF COMPASSION

SWEETEST TALES ARE THOSE that tell of saddest times. The saddest aspects of life give rise to compassion in the hearts of those who are self-realized. Thus compassion is a synthesis of both happiness and distress, for the compassionate are not unhappy themselves, but are unhappy for others while satisfied in their own lives.

This is the basis of the transcendent experience, a synthesis of polar opposites—good/bad, hot/cold, happiness/distress—that takes us above duality. Compassion is the heart of transcendence, and it is in enlightened consciousness that we can find the heart of compassion.

The distress of others provides the opportunity to lend a helping hand, and the joy derived from helping others is unparalleled. But to experience the highest joy, to get to the heart of compassion, we will have to know the extent of the suffering in this world and how to stop it. If we do not know the root cause of another's suffering, we may do that person more harm than good in attempting to alleviate his or her misery. If our baby cries because of too much gas in her stomach, but we think she is crying out of hunger, our good intentions and the best milk will have the worst effect.

According to the *Vedanta*, the reasoning of Indian philosophy, all the visible suffering of this world has an underlying, invisible cause. The disease of which hunger, epidemics, political oppression, environmental disaster, and violations of human and animal rights are symptoms, is called *maya*, or illusion. This illusion arises out of misidentification. As individual units of consciousness, *chit kana*, identify with matter, the veil of illusion is drawn. Perceiving the world through the medium of the senses, we

ANCIENT WISDOM

gather information and experience. As the senses of hearing, tasting, smelling, seeing, and touching contact their objects—sound, flavor, aroma, shape, and form—sensations are relayed to the mind. The mind either accepts or rejects these sensations, categorizing them as good or bad. Thus whether something tastes good or bad is relative; that is, it is not true in all instances. The same thing may taste delicious to you and unpalatable to me. So which is it? "Neither," *Vedanta* replies. The very sense of good or bad, happiness or distress, hot or cold, is illusory. Through the mind and senses, consciousness creates an illusory world of good and evil. The purpose of spiritual culture is to take us beyond the purview of the mind and senses to see the true nature of reality. Thus we are said to be suffering from an identity crisis. The whole of our material experience is likened to a bad dream from which we need to awaken. Sri Chaitanya has referred to the task of awakening the sleeping masses to their spiritual prospect as *para upakara*, the best thing we can do for suffering humanity. Short of this, all measures to improve our present situation do not get to the root of the problem.

This basic theme can be elaborated on considerably. The *Vedanta* makes a very strong case, one that many Western thinkers have been forced to reckon with. Yet applying this logic seems almost inhuman. Are we to neglect the world we live in? How can we be spiritual, filled with divine love and compassion, and at the same time be insensitive to the suffering around us, ignoring it while absorbed in "meditation"?

How to harmonize the logic of *Vedanta* and our own humanness is a problem that any thoughtful and caring person must deal with. Solving this problem is tantamount to self-realization. It involves understanding our human condition as the final stage in our evolution toward enlightenment, and human compassion as a shadow of the substance of absolute compassion, a shadow we need to pass through on our way to transcendence. Any approach to ultimate transcendence that does not deal thoroughly with this dilemma will keep us tied to mundanity, even while surrounded by spiritual trappings.

There are two basic pitfalls on the spiritual path, two erroneous conceptions that arise in attempting to deal with this crucial issue. The first leaves one hard-hearted, the second renders one illogical.

Insensitivity to the plight of others sometimes predominates in those who have formally adopted a spiritual path. Using the logic of the scriptures and repeating the words of the *rishis* can be abused to insulate one from one's own inner inadequacies in genuinely caring for others on the human level. This amounts to confusing genuine detachment (a very high state of consciousness) with indifference to the suffering of others. The difficulties others face are viewed rather coolly by this first group as "tough karma." "People are getting what they deserve, reaping what they themselves have sown." No doubt this is true; however, merely adopting the reasoning and language of enlightenment is insufficient. It does not a compassionate soul make.

Living in a monastery atop the Himalayas is often thought of as the ultimate spiritual cop-out. And it may be for many who are not yet able to embrace the spiritual path wholeheartedly—those who are trying to escape their lack of caring by hiding behind the robes of renunciation. In the words of Anthony, Ecker, and Wilber in *Spiritual Choices*, theirs is "an epistemological sleight-of-hand by claiming an existential point of view which is not, in fact, authentic for him or her. The follower's consciousness is still heavily conditioned by pleasure and pain, joy and sorrow. An honest orientation would involve concern and empathy for the suffering of others, and, while accepting suffering as a result of karma, would view karmic determination as a process that one is not yet able to fully understand or apply to the problem of suffering." Adopting the dress of a renunciate is not enough; one must become a truly caring person on all levels.

When fully developed, the transcendentalists will naturally choose to apply their caring where it will do the most good. At the same time a spiritually evolved person cannot but shed a tear for the pain others feel on the human level. The enlightened souls may not spend their time opening hospitals, but they genuinely care about the suffering of others. This is possible for them because of their genuine detachment, which allows them full involvement in all circumstances without karmic repercussions.

There are those who are evolved enough to adopt the path of renunciation and deal with the root cause of suffering directly, few though they may be. They dwell in the heart of compassion. But we, either as beginners in the *ashrama* or persons living in the world, cannot artificially adopt the view of the fully enlightened and not be culpable of neglecting our duty to the world and others on the human level. Thus, although there is a platform of ultimate compassion, there is also imitation, or mere intellectual adherence to this concept. The latter is a psychological maneuver for coping that will not help us very much, while the former is the goal of transcendent consciousness. This goal is attained through the gradual development of the compassionate heart.

One who is not ready for a life of renunciation should not live in a monastery. But if one wants to reach the heart of compassion, one must do more than help humanity, for without sensual restraint and stilling the mind one will never know the dimension of the soul. This leads us to the second misconception—rationalizing away one's inability to adhere to spiritual practices and leaving the *ashrama* to "help the world."

It is not enough to help others who are suffering in the world. Feeding and clothing the poor, opening hospitals, and speaking out against political oppression do not add up to enlightenment. Spiritual practices such as controlling the senses, yoga, meditation, and chanting the names of God involve the inner development of the soul. These kinds of activities, when engaged in under the direction of a self-realized spiritual guide, awaken realized knowledge of the nature of the self and the world around us. Philanthropy and altruism cannot replace meditation. They are in fact tinged with the mud of mundanity. They are extended forms of ego-gratification, which reach beyond immediate bodily gratification and cater to the subtle form of our material condition, the mental system. The good feeling we get from feeding the poor, for example, is often based on our mental conception of what the world is (as understood through the medium of the senses), a notion that is sure to be mistaken. It gratifies our illusory conception of the self. It is a subtle form of self-centeredness. Even if we see others' suffering as our own, not admitting to the illusion of separateness we live in, we experience at best an underdeveloped spirituality, for in this condition one has yet to gain acquaintance with his or her spiritual individuality as a servant of Godhead.

The work of God is not to help the poor any more than it is to help the rich, not to help the sick anymore than to help those who are healthy. In fact the rich and healthy may be more in need of God's help, proud as they often are of their pennies and push-ups. Equating philanthropic works with ultimate spirituality is a common misconception that arises in dealing with the harmonizing of the head and heart. Living in the monastery yet unable to practice the discipline or feeling the need to be involved with the world such that one's practices are constantly disturbed is certainly justification for leaving the mountain top. Yet it is easy to rationalize one's material attachments, thinking that by leaving and, say, working for the blind, one is opening the eyes of others to the ignorance of misidentification (*maya*). In fact, one may be facilitating the prolongation of another's life in illusion. Such persons should leave the *ashrama*, yet understand their shortcomings and be careful not to justify their actions, equating their inadequacies with the work of the enlightened.

Spiritual life unfolds gradually. We cannot jump to the highest platform, ignoring the nature and degree of our material conditioning. We cannot equate spiritual life with fact-gathering; spiritual life must translate into action. It is indeed a cop-out to espouse the philosophy of *Vedanta* but not care for the suffering of others. But it is also a cop-out to equate our material identification and desire for material interaction with the work of enlightened consciousness. Those practicing spiritual life who cannot leave the world behind and rationalize their leaving the monastery or their practice for the sake of doing philanthropic work are as guilty of pseudospirituality as the false renunciates.

The heart of compassion ultimately lies in enlightenment. The work of the enlightened soul is not opening hospitals. It is curing the disease of misidentification by broadcasting the message of transcendence, while genuinely caring for the suffering of others. Reaching this goal is no easy task: it requires that we carefully practice spiritual discipline while assessing the degree to which we are still under the jurisdiction of karma, the law of this world. Honest assessment of our condition will then dictate our responsibility

THE HEART OF COMPASSION

to worldly affairs. Gradually, with spiritual guidance, we can pass through (not skip over or get stuck in) human compassion and arrive at the inner heart of compassion. It is here that real caring takes place based on knowledge of what is worth caring about and what the ultimate cause of suffering is.

The boy-saint Prahlad of the *Bhagavat Purana* is an example of the heart of compassion. Once self-realized, he thought not to leave the world but to remain and attend to the deliverance of all other living entities from the mire of illusion. Buddha, Shankara, Christ, Sri Chaitanya, and many others also stand out as examples in the history of the world. They cared for the sufferings of others, but their time was principally spent in their own spiritual cultivation and subsequently disseminating transcendental knowledge and advocating love of God. Their view was decidedly that service to God is the highest service to humankind, not that service to humankind is the last word in service to Godhead.

The element of higher compassion in transcendence is a logical necessity. If it does not exist, the balance of good and evil that all caring people seek is not to be found, for as long as we remain within the world of sense perception, *our* good will always be an evil for someone else.

Genuine spirituality is not an icy act of world-denying, nor is it a flaky sentimental embracing of the problems of others without knowledge of an overall solution to their suffering. It is a caring based on knowledge, a spiritual emotion, if you will. There is a transcendental status of neutrality beyond worldly love and hate, a higher synthesis that cancels out the material duality. And it is this state that we endeavor for through philanthropic and altruistic efforts, attempting to bring balance to our world. We seek it, but how close do we come to it by the everyday means of lend-ing a helping hand? Only as far as we understand that through such world-serving activity our work is all for naught. That is, it will never permanently change the world. Thus the value of such work is not in that it improves a world where death is the norm, but that it softens the heart, enabling us to pass through material compassion to transcendental knowledge.

As long as the heart is stonelike and one cannot shed a tear for not only the plight of humanity but all species, there is no question of developing the pure heart of spiritual compassion. Ram Dass has explained it thus: "There are many levels of heart. And the human heart will break because it empathizes. The deeper heart—the *hridayam*, the *jivatma*, or the *hsin hsin* in Chinese—that heart is the one that looks at the universe just as it is, in a non-reactive way, and says, 'Ah so, yes.' And it includes your own human heart which is breaking, but your identity isn't only with your human heart. Your identity is with a deeper intuitive heart wisdom which is different."

Self-realized souls are usually not involved in helping others in their various predicaments in this world because they do not see the suffering as we do. They are also too busy serving the need of those ready to hear about the ultimate solution to material suffering.

A few years ago, during a speaking tour I did in Eastern Europe, a young man from Bulgaria asked me, "Does your mission of meditation and self-realization do anything for the suffering of the world? What does it do practically to solve the world's problems?" I replied, "The difference between you and I is that you think that the world *has* problems, whereas I think that the 'world', as you see it, *is* the problem." For the self-realized soul, everything is moving in accordance with the will of God. Let well enough alone, and inform others that everything is all right. The only thing lacking is acquiring the proper angle of vision.

Once one of my godbrothers asked our guide if he could render any service. To this our mentor replied, "Change your angle of vision; this is real service." Hunger, for example, is not a stomach problem, it is a disease of the heart. As long as we insist on viewing the world through the limited and imperfect instruments of sense perception, we live in a world we have created, *not* the kingdom of God. We live where one living being is food for another, where exploitation is the norm. We create friends and enemies and perpetuate our suffering.

Just as the suffering of a son after his first childhood heartbreak is not something to take very seriously, so the suffering of humanity is not what it is made out to be by those who are presently troubled by it. One who sees the soul in all circumstances knows that the future of the struggling living entities is bright. Our human suffering, however long it endures, is insignificant when compared to eternity. However many lifetimes it may take to tread the path of eternality amounts to but a few moments of our real life. It is all a dream soon to be forgotten, a sad tale that tells, if we look very closely, of sweeter times.

DEMYSTIFYING MYSTIC POWERS

THERE WAS A TIME WHEN answers to the majority of the questions about human nature and the world we live in were considered unknowable. Many of the workings of material nature that we understand today were at one time explained as miracles.

In the field of medicine, *ad hoc* cures requiring "divine intervention" have today been replaced with routine medical procedures performed by practitioners of a different faith. Modern science has systematically demystified much of the world. But there are many mysteries yet to be explained. The supernatural powers possessed by advanced practitioners of yoga are one example.

The subject of mystic power always draws an audience. The recently published *Modern Miracles* of Dr. Erlendur Haraldsson, in which Dr. Haraldsson undertakes an investigative study of the psychic phenomena surrounding Sai Baba, an Indian mystic famous for displays of magical powers, was sold out almost everywhere I tried to purchase it.

In India, yogis have been exhibiting mystic feats for centuries and many of their accomplishments have been documented. The ancient literature of that country is filled with accounts of persons possessing supernatural powers. This information often fascinates Westerners, and even today anyone with sufficient interest can go to the Himalayan foothills and observe the wonderful prowess of India's yogis. Many people are doing just that in search of power through yoga.

ANCIENT WISDOM

The *siddhis*, or mystic powers, of yogis are many and of varying degrees. At a glance they are quite desirable. Would you like to be able to change your shape at will, appear in up to eight different places simultaneously or suddenly turn invisible? Who hasn't desired to know the future or read another's mind? What about attaining bodily strength like that of an elephant without having to look like Mr. America? Care to talk with other species? These are all only a few of the secondary yogic perfections. Shall I go on?

Unlike the above mentioned feats, which are also common to various indigenous cultures and shamanistic in nature, the yoga system speaks of eight mystic perfections (*ashta siddhi*), which upon achieving one is often thought to have attained Godhood. In his *Yoga Sutras*, Patanjali Muni distinguishes these mystic perfections from the above mentioned lesser yogic perfections.

In India it is common for people who are only slightly accomplished in mystic yoga to advertise themselves as God. Aside from the fact that the idea of *becoming* God seems to contain inherently contradictory notions, these *siddhis* are indeed extraordinary, bordering Godliness, at least in the sense of God's power potential. However, God, it would seem, is much more than merely powerful. Perhaps his lovable aspect, his beauty and charm, is his better side, something not concomitant with the attainment of mystic power. Rather mystic power accompanies Godhead incidentally.

It is more accurate to say that accomplished yogis are merely tapping into their own mystic power rather than becoming God. After all, the living force is a mystery. How is it that a lemon tree can produce citric acid? Life producing chemicals; it is a mystery. So much so that scientists are trying to prove the opposite: life comes from chemicals.

DEMYSTIFYING MYSTIC POWERS

What is the ingredient that makes matter come to life? What is the power of the living force? Can anyone explain it? In this sense every soul has mystic power. The yoga system simply develops the mystic power already present in the practitioner. It doesn't turn the practitioner into God.

Before we discuss the eight *maha siddhis*, let's examine the dynamics of yogic attainment by which any of the above mentioned supernatural powers are acquired. The yogic model of the mind is different than that of modern science. In the scientific community the mind is really nothing more than neurological eruptions, another part of our biophysical makeup. Modern psychology is considered the study of the mind, but for the most part it seeks to cure mental disease by prescribing chemicals that affect the centers of the brain. In modern psychology, the mind is not an independent level of reality interacting with the body, rather it is a not yet very well understood aspect of our biology and ultimately our physiology. Parapsychologists and perhaps transpersonal psychologists are venturing on to what science would term thin ice—the study of the mind as an independent level of our reality, independent of our body.

While psychology explores the conscious mind in dream and waking states and the unconscious or subconscious aspect of the mind as well, yoga deals with still another dimension of the mind—the superconscious level. Yoga is the complete science of the mind (although when we use the term "science" it must be understood in terms of its etymology and not merely the severely limited notions it conjures up in our present day and age). The prevailing "scientific" outlook recognizes psychology due to psychology's willingness to conform to the existing scientific framework, whereas parapsychology and now perhaps transpersonal psychology are seen as renegade quackery.

ANCIENT WISDOM

And yoga, the complete science of the mind, is yet to be distinguished in some Western minds from its dietary associate, yogurt.

In yoga terminology *samyama* refers to mental exercise that awakens the superconscious and thus supernatural ability, which is only supernatural in terms of the popular conception of "natural," i.e. observable physical events. Seen otherwise (in terms of a broader conception of the nature of life) these powers are considerably demystified.

Before being able to perform *samyama*, the yoga practitioner must pass through five external processes: forming an ethical foundation (*yama* and *niyama*), mastering sitting postures (*asana*), controlling the breath (*pranayama*), and withdrawing attention from sense objects (*pratyahara*). *Samyama* refers to the last three aspects of the eightfold yoga system: *dharana*, *dhyana* and *samadhi*. These three stages are so similar that they overlap one another. Thus while practicing *dharana* (concentration) one slips into *dhyana* (meditation) and *samadhi* (trance). Because these three are so similar, their threefold practice is addressed singularly as *samyama*.

When one's conscious mind is peaceful (undisturbed by the senses and their objects) and one's subconscious is subdued, one can perform *samyama*. The very nature of the mind is to penetrate an object, as this writer's mind is penetrating both the subject and the mind of the reader. By exercising *samyama* on a particular object, the object is penetrated in a heightened sense resulting in comprehension of the object *en toto*. Thus the essence of that object becomes known.

For example, when yogis perform *samyama* concentrating on hot coals, not only do they come to know the phenomenon of combustion, but they are able to identify the

DEMYSTIFYING MYSTIC POWERS

psychochemical process of combustion in the coals with that of the "fire" in the human body as well as that of the sun. The yogis thus penetrate the nature of fire on three levels, the astral (sun), the biological (human body), and the physical (the coals). They then reduce these three to a common denominator—material nature as the fire element. Their mental absorption on the material element of fire results in full *comprehension,* or mastery of fire. Yogis therefore find no difficulty walking on fire.

The *Yoga Sutras* describe the relationships between various pairs of objects and what corresponding supernatural power one can attain by performing *samyama* on those objects. Thus by *samyama* on the relationship of body and space, one achieves levitation. By *samyama* on physical changes, changes in character, and changes of states of the world, one achieves knowledge of the past and future. By *samyama* on word analysis, one can understand the intentions of all species. By *samyama* on the psychic mechanism, one can read others' minds. By *samyama* on the form and color of the body, the yogi can disappear at will. By *samyama* on power, one achieves great strength, and by *samyama* on the sun, one gains knowledge of the universe. These are but a few examples outlined in the *Sutras*. Some discussion of these powers may reveal a practical side to them, thus demystifying them even in terms of the material conception of life. With regard to the *maha siddhis,* we will also attempt to see through the mystery of their mastery or at least examine their usefulness, thus putting them in proper perspective.

LEVITATION

Within our bodies there are many electromagnetic forces, which are the same forces that govern other objects within space up to the stars and planets. The earth is said to move, despite its weight and massive size, at a rate of nineteen miles per second. It moves so, as do the other planets, on account of its being directly connected to gravitational and electromagnetic forces. Our bodies are indirectly connected with these forces. If we can directly connect our bodies with these forces through *samyama*, the power to travel in space is achieved.

Besides this physical levitation there is psychic levitation. Of the two, the latter is more important. If the psyche is in levitation (centered on elevating thoughts) this upward movement of the mind enables one to overcome physical attractions, which are the cause of suffering. When mental levitation slackens, one is maladjusted. When it is heightened one can function psychically at the speed of mind and travel faster than the speed of light. As the mind can go anywhere in a moment, so the yogi can mount the mental chariot and tangibly experience distant places.

KNOWLEDGE OF PAST, PRESENT AND FUTURE

The study of cause and effect is the infallible method of psychological analysis. The cause can be inferred from its effect while the effect can be understood from its cause. By studying the present, which is the effect of the past, one can know about one's past. Similarly, by knowing the present, which is the cause of the future effect, one can know what is yet to come. Through merging cause into effect and effect into cause, the yogi finds continuity, and thus time is transcended.

As the body can move in any direction in space, so the mind can move in any direction, not only in space but in time as well. The body can move forward in time as seen in the aging process, but it cannot move backward in time. The mind, however, can move backward in time, as it were, as in the case of mental regression wherein one "relives" one's childhood.

DEMYSTIFYING MYSTIC POWERS

MIND READING

The mind is not bound by corporal laws. The psyche, which controls the movements of the body, also determines how the mind works. If one knows the laws that govern the mind, one can know others' minds in the same way that one knows one's own mind. People cannot read others' minds only because they cannot read their own.

Through deductive and inductive inference, one can also read minds to some extent. This is the method pursued by the psychoanalysts, who penetrate the minds of their patients. Again, it can be said that penetration is the very nature of the mind. Thus one who masters one's own mental faculty can penetrate the minds of others.

INVISIBILITY

There are many things that we cannot see although they are all around us. Vision of anything depends on the eyes receiving the reflection of light from the object of sight. Without that reflection, objects remain invisible. The body is made up of atoms. It becomes visible to the eye of another because it possesses color, which is reflected in the presence of light. If one can check the perception of the color of the body by reducing the threshold of the perception of reflective light, one can in effect disappear.

MAHA SIDDHIS

The *maha siddhis* are also referred to as *ashta siddhi* or eight mystic powers. These eight are particularly singled out from other lesser powers, which are but partial manifestations of the same.

Anima is the power to make oneself small, so much so that one can enter into the atom or *anu* (smallest particle). *Laghima* is the power to make oneself lighter than air. Levitation is a partial development of this *siddhi*. *Mahima* or *garima* refers to the power to make oneself large, to expand in space, or to become heavy and immovable. *Prapti siddhi* refers to the ability to "touch the moon" or to acquire items from distant places. *Prapti* literally means "acquisition." Yogis are often known for their ability to "manifest" out-of-season fruits or small items of jewelry. This is really the power of acquisition rather than the power to manifest something from nothing. *Ishita* is the power to create or destroy at will. *Vashita* is the power not only to penetrate and know others' minds but to control others' minds as well. *Prakamya* is the ability to create wonderful effects within the scope of nature, and *kamavasayita* refers to the power to do things that contradict nature. All of these *siddhis* are indeed wonderful, yet on closer scrutiny it is apparent that they are not as desirable as one might think. This is in fact the statement of Patanjali Muni himself. These powers are really only side effects of the practice of yoga and not the goal. They are not something to be sought after, for if that is one's intention, the pursuit of God consciousness will be checked, and God consciousness, or union in love of God, is the very goal of yoga.

Modern science, our doubting Thomas, might consider that the accomplishments of the mystic yogis are the perfection of many of science's pursuits on the gross material plane. Most of the eight great *siddhis* have already been accomplished by modern technology to some extent. *Anima*, for example, the ability to enter into stone, has been achieved in the form of excavating the earth through which man mines valuable minerals and creates subways (now homes for America's homeless, especially during the winter months).

Laghima, the power to walk on water and become lighter than air, has also been accomplished by modern technology, which can float huge ships across vast oceans and fly heavy machinery high in the sky. Similarly, in

DEMYSTIFYING MYSTIC POWERS

relation to acquisition (*prapti siddhi*), thanks to modern technology, what item from any distant place is not available for the person who has a sufficient bank balance? In America have we not become accustomed to enjoying fruits that not to speak of being out of season here, do not even grow in our country? Modern technology has made both the world smaller and our experience greater. Some see this as a kind of "spirituality." Actually, following this course leads to just the opposite—worldliness—as is the case with the pursuit of similar powers in the extended context of yoga.

The ability of the yogi to control the minds of others, *vashita*, by which many who are partially accomplished in the art speak nonsense and enamor the less intelligent with pseudo "yoga philosophy," has been perfected perhaps even more by modern man than any yogi. George Orwell's "1984" has come and gone leaving us with a sigh of relief. But Aldous Huxley's *Brave New World* has come to pass. The "medium is *more* than the message," and that's not such good news. Just turn on the television. Who's in charge? It would be prudent to suggest that we not underestimate the mystic power of the nightly newscast.

Practically there are parallels in the modern world of all the mystic accomplishments, although admittedly they are for the most part manifest in crude form. This observation, however, should serve to help demystify mystic powers, which amount to nothing more than the soul's inherent power to *subtly* manipulate matter. At the same time, exploring the potential subtle power of the soul may lead to a greater appreciation of the soul itself and from there to fulfillment. In light of this, it would be wise for modern men and women to reconsider the materialist conception of reality that they foolishly wave with the flag of empiricism.

ANCIENT WISDOM

The soul unfettered by the gross and subtle material coverings has immense power. Its full expression is not the power to control and manipulate matter and mind but the power to love. The power to love is achieved when one learns to love God—which is the very goal of yoga.

OLD AGE COMMON SENSE FOR NEW AGE NONSENSE

BY NOW THE TERM *new age* is part of the vocabulary of practically every American. A consistent definition of the term, however, is not as commonplace. For the most part, the new age—a label given by the media—isn't a specific group, rather it is a class of people of diverse interests united by common values.

Social-critic Marilyn Ferguson, whose best-seller *The Aquarian Conspiracy* has been dubbed "The Handbook of the New Age" by *USA Today*, sees a new age that has as its members those who espouse an underlying holistic philosophy. They attempt to see the interelationship of problems instead of mechanistically viewing each problem separately. They emphasize decentralization of power with the view to promote the development of whole individuals and tend to view things globally by keeping the long-range interests of the planet in mind.

Ferguson sees many smaller movements and individuals as members of the much larger new age social phenomenon. Although it is often thought of as a movement arising out of a spiritual foundation, many of the major influences have come from humanistic psychology. For example, the human potential movement of the 1960s and 1970s, epitomized by psychologists like Carl Rogers and Abraham Maslow, is largely responsible for laying the foundation of the optimism that pervades new age thought.

The movement's spiritual credentials are questioned by Jonathon Adolph, senior editor of *New Age Magazine*. In an article written for the *1988 Guide to New Age Living*,

ANCIENT WISDOM

Adolph asserts that the claim that spirituality underlies the new age phenomenon has been problematic and "a source of much confusion regarding the new age in general." He says, "The new age is not a religion," and he questions what is meant by spirituality by the many who loosely use the term.

However, the latest rising star on the new age horizon—trance channelers—have difficulty with the aforementioned concept of the new age. They would like to deify the new age. Although the more down-to-earth, humanistic new age advocates recognize the "new spiritualists" to be members of the new age family, more and more they are seeking to disassociate themselves from them, giving them a place on the fringe. Much to the embarrassment of long-standing members, the media recently has given more attention to this "fringe" element than it has to the entire new age movement in the last decade.

Recently, *Time* magazine dedicated its cover story to the new age, starring Shirley MacLaine. The thrust of the article dealt with the latest booming industries within the new age—channeling and crystals—surrounded by an aura of wisdom from an "old age," which, ironically, new-agers say has gone by. Many may have thought it unfair for *Time* to have characterized the entire new age as a paranormal, quasi-spiritual good way to make a fast buck, but the fact is that millions of people *are* becoming enamored by the prospect of quick-fix cosmic cures to the problems facing humanity and others are cashing in on it.

What attracts people to the not-so-new spirituality is difficult to say. Channeling, for example, has been around since time immemorial. It has generally appealed to undereducated sections of society and is prominent in many third world countries. In Brazil it is known as Macumba, and although most of the country is officially Catholic, unofficially Macumba is practically the national

OLD AGE COMMON SENSE FOR NEW AGE NONSENSE

religion. While the poorer sections are open about it, the aristocratic class is equally involved behind closed doors. Haiti and many African nations are also heavily influenced by a kind of spiritualism involving channeling, and one would be hard-pressed to find a culture where its influence was altogether absent.

Channeling was also spoken of by the Greek philosophers Plato, Aristotle, and Socrates. Some say that those channeled insights had much to do with the shaping of the basic principles of Western law. President Lincoln invited the famous medium Andrew Jackson Davis to the White House and his channeled information inspired Lincoln to sign the Emancipation Proclamation. Channelers tell us that the popularity of channeling in America today is due to the fertile combination of breakthrough information and people now ready for enlightenment, people whose time has come.

Leaving aside the American way of marketing as another possibility of channeling's popularity, it is true that the kind of information that new age people receive from channeled entities is different than the information sought after and received in many third world countries. Global prophecies, stock market predictions, and technological insights, for example, have replaced information about finding lost loves, catching unfaithful partners, and speaking with deceased relatives. Moreover, the new information is about a spiritual time to come and a new spirituality: a new age. Just how accurate the new information is, however, is subject to suspicion, especially when it contradicts many of the spiritual truths held over the centuries by persons of exemplary character.

Several popular channeled entities have labeled the traditional transcendentalists who have walked among us as members of the "old spiritual age." Although it is commonly understood that actions speak louder than words,

ANCIENT WISDOM

these disembodied new age leaders, while speaking at considerable length, remain in such a state that their actions cannot be observed. In fact, the channelers themselves generally insist that they cannot be held accountable for their own actions!

The "old spiritual age," however, has already spoken of channeling and the method by which the physically embodied can approach the disembodied, as well as what kind of result such communication can be expected to produce. Throughout revealed scripture in every major religious tradition, channeling is referred to. The Old Testament considers channelers to be bad company. "Let no one be found among you who sacrifices his son or daughter in the fire, who practices divination or sorcery, interprets omens, engages in witchcraft or casts spells, or *who is a medium or spiritualist* or consults the dead" (Deuteronomy 18:10,11). And in the *Bhagavad-Gita* we find: "Those who worship the demigods will take birth among the demigods; those who worship the ancestors go to the ancestors; those who worship ghosts and spirits will take birth among such beings; and those who worship me will live with me." (Bg. 9.25). From this sampling of verses it would appear that in the opinion of "the old spiritual age" channeling is somewhat less than divine.

Of course, channeling as it is known today is not to be confused with the inspired side of a saint through which revealed scripture is manifested. The willingness of God to move the pen of humanity depends on humanity's utter willingness to serve the will of God, devoid of any tinge of self-interest. The pens of the apostles of Christ; the inspired writings of Vyasadeva, the author of the *Vedas;* and Mohammed's *Koran* have left the world with timeless wisdom. Their inspired followers exemplify a wholesale dedication to the inspired word and its singular author whose message appears in various forms in accordance with time and circumstances. Possessed of that spirit, saints are capable of shedding new light on the revealed truth; new light not in the sense of throwing out the words that have come before, but merely shining a brighter light on the same words. By the sun's light, the rose comes into bloom. That, however, is a far cry from replacing the rose with a dandelion, as the channelers have attempted to do.

According to the *Vedas,* the mental world is the background of the physical realm. It is like a vast body of water, and the physical world can be compared to ice. Ice is a temporary transformation of water under certain conditions. The mental plane is far more accommodating than the physical. For example, if we look around the room we're in, we see so many objects. But how many of them can we physically carry? In the mind, however, we can carry everything in the room with us wherever we go. It is said that work is done in the mind. It is only later carried out through the senses. The mind is more subtle than the body but more powerful. The mental world, however, is not the divine world. God knows what evil lurks in the minds of men . . . (and most of us have some idea as well).

Above the mind is the intelligence, the power of discrimination. Although with the help of the mind I may determine that something is pleasing, with the help of the intelligence I may determine that it may not really be good for me. The height of intellectual exercise is to discriminate between spirit and matter. That may give us a glimpse of the soul. The intellect may lead us to the soul, but its capacity to guide is limited. Intellect is but a servant of the soul, and the soul is but a servant of God.

What kind of information can we get from the mental world? The only thing we can be sure of is that it will not be one hundred percent accurate most of the time. It is certainly not absolute.

ANCIENT WISDOM

There are many types of inhabitants in the mental realm ranging from benevolent to demoniac, from progressive to regressive. It stands to reason that the kind of entities that are most easy to get in touch with are those who are themselves attached to the physical plane. These would be entities who are possessed of physical material desires yet whose *karma* would not allow them to acquire a physical form. For example, suicide is said to produce the karmic reaction of having to take birth in the mental world where there are no physical bodies. These entities remain hovering in an ethereal form, seeking opportunities to possess a body through which they can satisfy their desires. Similarly, those who do the work of channeling—the "gifted"—were most likely living in the mental world in their last life (there is a kind of death in the mental world); thus, their consciousness is still attached to that plane.

Those who are not grossly materially attached but still derive pleasure from having their views heard and appreciated solely for the sake of their own aggrandizement are subtly materially attached. Philosophers and thinkers, speculators and the like, who live in the mental plane can easily acquire a large audience here. Their views are no more profound, however, than many of the thoughtful persons from this plane, although they generally have more knowledge of the physical world. Thus most spirits can capture our attention by telling us about our past or something of the future.

In exchange for the satisfaction the spirits derive from our listening to them and taking their advice, those of an altruistic disposition often give practical help in many areas. In the fields of medicine, invention, science, investment, or in just helping one to feel good about oneself, there is plenty of documented evidence that the disembodied can be helpful. Edgar Cayce provided consistently accurate

OLD AGE COMMON SENSE FOR NEW AGE NONSENSE

medical data, although he knew little or nothing about medicine in his waking state. Lazarus of Concept Synergy currently gives a pretty good sermon about PMA (positive mental attitude), but that is about as far as it goes. Beyond that, many spirit guides get in over their auras, especially when they contradict genuine spiritual traditions, which have produced numerous saints on earth.

An example of such contradiction is found in a popular theme of channeled guides, Westernized reincarnation. According to some new trance channelers, we can only progress. There is no question of falling back to a lower lifeform. But the literature of ancient India, wherein the process of reincarnation was originally described, does not lend itself to such interpretation. The idea that we can only progress does not even match with our experience or common sense. If a man is given a high and responsible position along with certain privileges and facilities and misuses them, as did, say, Richard Nixon, he will be hurled down or impeached.

Therefore, we must seriously consider that today's popular channeled entities are not divine but rather mental or astral, and thus cannot bring their audiences to the highest destination sought by genuine spiritual seekers since the beginning of recorded history.

If the more humanistic section of the new-agers are embarrassed by the many who have attempted to make divinity out of the paranormal, they have no one to blame but themselves. Humanism, after all, is nothing but the speculative attempt to equate humanity with divinity, and a man-made God is no God at all. Such a heretical idea of spirituality can never satisfy the souls of humanity. We should call a spade a spade, especially in this instance. Otherwise, we become subject to potential contempt of the Supreme. This in turn may threaten our chances of ever achieving the

ANCIENT WISDOM

harmonious life, which, regardless of how much we herald its arrival, still continues to elude us. In the words of Plutarch, "It is better to have no opinion about God at all than such a one as is unworthy of Him: for the one is only unbelief—the other is contempt."

The license to speculate can be dangerous. Just as in mechanistic science there are certain axiomatic truths, so also in nonmechanistic science, or spiritual science, there are fundamental axiomatic truths. For example, that the soul lies beyond the limited conceptions of race, sex, nationality, and so on is an axiomatic truth. We are moved to question, therefore, when our cultural, sexual, or social orientation gets the upper hand in shaping our "spirituality." Do we have the liberty to create new spiritual axioms in the name of enlightened thinking? Until our behavior is at least in accordance with the saints who have come before us in traditional religion, a grain of caution may be wise.

Everyone has the inalienable right to pursue enlightenment at their own pace and of their own volition (necessarily), and there is tremendous scope for new revelation even within God-given traditional religious systems. From Shankara to Ramanuja to Madhva to Sri Chaitanya, from Old Testament to New, there are many examples of this. We must look not to replace the law but to fulfill it. Too often speculative theories regarding the nature of spirituality expose themselves as uninformed opinions when they blame "shortcomings" in the "old age of spirituality" for their necessity to redefine divinity. In the words of Bernadette Roberts, author of *The Experience of No Self,* "The inclusiveness of the traditional paths is well attested to by the contemplatives who never went 'outside' of their religion to see the divine in all that exists—or see all that exists as a manifestation of the divine. To overlook this fact is indicative of an out-of-hand rejection of traditional religion by those who have obviously never lived it. That some people choose not to go the traditional route is their prerogative, but to blame their choice on a deficit in traditional religion is contrary to the fact and totally absurd."

Our conjectures about the nature of Godhead must arise out of a strong foundation, one which has been laid down by saints and scriptures in previous times. Enlightened thinking requires that we are careful not to throw out the baby with the bath water. If we are truly interested in enlightened thinking, the planet is rich with examples from every religious tradition from which to draw inspiration. Is it enlightened thinking to feel that it is beneath our dignity to follow greater thinkers who have gone before us? Do not the greatest of thinkers advocate that we also think for ourselves? When so many saints have already come before us leading the way, perhaps it is only our lack of courage and utter attachment to this earthly plane that has forced us to come up with "new ideas" about spiritual life, which may amount to no more than self-deception and relative improvements of character. No one can deny the noble character of Christ or the idea that a society of Christ-like men and women would undoubtedly be a new age, but very, very few are courageous enough to follow such an example. Very few are thoroughly convinced of the dire necessity for a *truly* new age.

Genuine spirituality remains above the mental and intellectual conjectures of much of the new age speculation, as something not to be known except by those who follow the guidelines by which God allows himself to be known. This is not a discrimination on his part, but an invitation on his terms. Although those terms may appear to be restricting for the neophyte, it is not the self that they seek to restrict, but the demands of the material coverings of the soul in the form of the body and mind for which we maintain a deep affection. If we love our vehicle so much that we let it take us in the wrong direction, we may end up in a fool's paradise. But if we steer our vehicle in the direction pointed to by genuine saints—past and present—then we can actually achieve the divine consciousness that trance channelers and humanists fall short of producing in their followers.

If there is indeed a new age upon us, it is found in those calling for the visions of the enlightened to descend within us. It is a group that sees the frailties of humanity and seeks communion with the divine. It is the finite drawing the sympathy of the infinite. It is a new generation wholeheartedly following the genuine spiritual traditions of the past and finding new inspiration in doing so. It is admittedly a time for the most part yet to come, but a time which will be truly worthy of the title *new age*.

HALLOWED BE THY NAME

EVERY RELIGIOUS TRADITION of the world maintains that the name of God is inherently sacred. Although God is addressed variously, the concept of the "holy name" of God is well known to all. Well known perhaps, but not very well understood. Most traditions speak of the sacredness of the divine name only in passing, but India's sacred scriptures elaborate on the rationale behind the concept of sacred sound, the most holy of which is considered to be the name of God.

But before we discuss communion with Godhead through sound, it will be prudent to first cross this hurdle: people often want to know if anyone has *seen* God. Thus before we can enter into a discussion about hearing and vibrating the name of God, it may be helpful to first put in proper perspective the relative value of our senses' capacity to perceive. Some may say "seeing is believing," but what we see may not be the real picture. If we had to rely solely on our senses (thank God we don't), we would be better off relying on our ears rather than our eyes. Let us examine just how important hearing and sound are to us, something we do not often stop to think about. Perhaps this can help us to appreciate how we may know God and perfect our lives through sound. It is not as farfetched an idea as one might think.

Hearing precedes practically all of our activities. Because we've heard about something we go to see it, after which we talk about it to others. Because we have heard from those whom we accept as authorities, we accept things as true even when we ourselves cannot verify them. No other sense can register stimulus as minimal as can our

ANCIENT WISDOM

sense of hearing. The extent of vibratory movement of our eardrum is 10^9. This is shorter than a wavelength of visible light, and less than the diameter of a hydrogen atom. The highest volume perceivable by the ear is the least audible sound multiplied 10^6. If we were to factor the smallest impulses perceivable by the eyes by the same power, we would be instantly blinded.

Hans Kayser, the founder of the scientific study of harmonies, has pointed out in his book *Akroasis* that the ears are the only human sense that can perceive numerical proportions and values simultaneously: "The ears not only recognize exact numerical proportions, that is, numerical quantities like 1:2 as an octave, 2:3 as a fifth, 3:4 as a fourth, etc.; at the same time they hear . . . values that they perceive as C, G, F, and so on. So the tone value fuses two elements into one unit: the element of sensing—the tone, that is—with the element of thinking, of numerical value. And this happens in such an exact manner that the value of the tone can be checked precisely against the value of the number, and the value of the number against the value of the tone. Among all our human senses we have only one organ that is capable of this fusion: the ears. In this way sensation controls deliberation—or to put it differently: our soul is capable of deciding on the correctness or incorrectness of an intellectual quantity. Conversely, the phenomenon of tone value also gives us the opportunity to develop proportions and numerical values in the realm of the psyche."

Bent as we are on seeing God, it is important to note that with our eyes we can only gather approximate data. Of course this is true of all of our senses, but among them the ear is the most precise and accurate. By differentiating between color tones with our eyes we can be nowhere near as exact as we can be with our ears in distinguishing between notes on the scale.

As hearing is important to us, so is sound. Yet we hardly think of sound as anything more than something that pleases or displeases our ears. Modern science, however, has in recent times lent support to the vision of the ancient *rishis* with regard to the sages' perception of "the world as sound." It has been widely accepted by the scientific community since the time of the physicist DeBroglie that the interactions of atomic particles can be treated entirely as wavelike motions. Atoms are not solid in the literal sense. The subatomic particles that make up atoms vibrate in space at distinct vibrational frequencies (called harmonics). In addition, all forms of energy are now considered vibrational in nature; for example, electromagnetic energy, which includes light, heat, radio waves, and so on, vibrate. Each of these energy forms are but different frequencies of the same wave. Does this concept not serve as scientific confirmation of the view of the *rishis?* The *world* is sound, and we are but a note!

Although hearing and sound are important to us, more important still is to listen. As good as the ear is, it is faulty like the rest of our material senses. But it can serve as an instrument for *listening*, which ultimately lies in the jurisdiction of the heart. Hearing and uttering the divine name is a heart exercise that requires dedication. If we examine the principle of dedication, we will better be able to understand the concept of divine sound.

Although it is generally accepted among transcendentalists that consciousness is foundational to our existence, dedication is a qualifier of consciousness that gets closer to the solution of life's mystery. Conscious we are; that is, possessed of will. Without will we cease to exist. Dedication is the inherent nature of the self. Everyone is serving something at every moment—country, community, family,

ANCIENT WISDOM

the mind's demands. Service implies choice or freedom, the most sought-after commodity.

To find the appropriate outlet in which to repose our serving tendency is thus the solution to our present predicament, for it should be fairly obvious to the honest seeker that at present the direction of our dedicating tendency has not resulted in ultimate fulfillment.

Dedication to the divine name brings fulfillment. Therefore, what do we mean when we speak of the holy name? It is not the physical sound or alphabetical representation that we utter with our tongue and hear with our ear. Uttering the name of God is not a lip exercise that can be performed by a parrot or tape recorder. The holy name is God incarnate in sound, and mere physical movements or mental exercise cannot attract the sympathy of the name. As we have will, so does the name, and God willing, we may receive the name proper through the medium of the saints. Those who carry within themselves the living conception of divine dedication can implant this conception within our hearts. From there the seed of the holy name grows. It appears on our lips and vibrates them, producing itself through the medium of our dedicated energy. As an electrical wire properly connected can produce light, so when we are properly oriented, we may vibrate the name of God and bring light to the world through divine sound.

It is necessary to differentiate the concept of vibrating and hearing the divine name and its effects upon the sincere spiritual aspirant from many of the popular sound inventions offered today for balancing our brain waves. Sometimes these inventions are advertised as capable of producing the same effect that previously took lifetimes of dedication and sacrifice to achieve, in a relatively short period of time—say, thirty minutes. Certain synchronized sound patterns, it may be demonstrated, produce a similar effect on the brain as that which is observed by researchers who study those who submit themselves to experimentation during meditation. Fine. But it is a long jump from there to the "thirty minutes" ads. We must remember that one's brain functioning similarly to another's says nothing about the similarity of their hearts. Such experiments may serve to inadvertently succumb to the reductionist worldview that the spiritual viewpoint repudiates. What's more, it is easy to understand how two opposite sources of stimuli can produce the same physical effect. Tears, for example, can be produced either from emotions of sadness or happiness.

God is more than mundane sound, and the sound that represents God in this world is not something we can manufacture in the recording studio. We may be able to produce many wonderful sounds, even ones that create, and there is no harm in such experimentation, but the experience of God consciousness is something that will have to descend to us from above. We need only to open our hearts to receive divine sounds.

When discussing the holy name, the Vedic literature—especially the purely devotional texts—mention many names of God. It would certainly be questionable if we were to limit the divine to but one name, especially when we ourselves have at least two and usually more. In the *Vedas* the many names of God are divided into two sections, primary and secondary. Secondary names are those which describe something about God's attributes in reference to a general presence in the world of *maya,* or illusion, such as *Brahman,* which refers to the underlying foundation, undifferentiated consciousness, out of which the *mayic* world arises. *Paramatma* is another such name, which refers to the Oversoul that accompanies the *jivatma,* or finite living being, throughout the material sojourn, and acts as a witness

ANCIENT WISDOM

to all of the *jivatma's* karmic deeds. Uttering secondary names of God attentively can bring liberation.

Direct names are those that refer to a more intimate concept of God as a divine being endowed with personal attributes and accompanied by innumerable associates and energies in transcendental abodes. These direct names of God are the object of considerable relish by those who have accepted that the name of God is sacred. Such votaries of the holy names are perhaps the best to look to for exploring this principle which, again, is mentioned universally throughout the religious world. That which is mentioned throughout is wholly applied by those engaged exclusively in the practice of chanting the name of God as a means of divine culture.

To this group of votaries, the uttering of the name is more than a means by which to achieve liberation. Although many others *do* chant primary names of God with a view to achieve liberation, theirs is not the culture of pure devotion per se. Theirs is the culture of knowledge mixed with devotion.

Those that vibrate the names of God to achieve liberation, thinking that any name of the divine is equal to any other, may encounter transcendence as a vague experience, like that of awakening from a deep sleep having experienced something that is tangible yet indescribable. Although they agree that the name is not physical sound, they maintain that it is mental and thus within the jurisdiction of illusion. Yet they believe that its incantation has the power to elevate one to the shore of transcendence, because it is of the material quality of goodness (*sattva guna*). Such transcendentalists (monists) contend that transcendence is formless and ultimately soundless. Their experience of transcendence, derived from culturing their particular conception of the name, is one of a homogeneous conscious substance, *Brahman*, which has no qualities or variety.

This understanding of transcendence is considered to be elementary by those who maintain that the divine name is a supramental sound representation of Godhead. The concept of a supramental name ascribes ultimate divinity to the name, which is considered to wholly correspond with the transcendental form of Godhead and a world of transcendental variegatedness. The logic of this transcendental viewpoint, as opposed to the idea of a soundless, formless absolute, may be better appreciated through the following example: As islands arise out of water in the sea from time to time, one may think that water is their origin; similarly, one may think that the world of temporary names and forms arises out of a undifferenciated sea of consciousness, only to disappear in due course. Yet the sea is not undifferenciated; there is life within the sea. To experience the world of consciousness as without variety is like describing the ocean as being wet—a rather shallow understanding of what makes up the sea. Actually the ocean consists of so many waves, what to speak of the world of sea life beneath her surface. As sea life is similar to but not the same as life on land, so the world of consciousness replete with forms and names is similar to but different from the world of material names and forms. As everything in the ocean is wet, so everything in the conscious world is conscious. Thus within the conception of a supramental name is an invitation to dive deep into the world of consciousness *(rasam anandam).*

For those engaged in *suddha bhakti* (pure devotion), vibrating the supramental name is both the means and the end of their culture of divinity. The form, qualities, and pastimes of Godhead are contained within the pure name. The perfection of the culture of the divine name lies in access-

ANCIENT WISDOM

ing the spiritual realm and participating in the divine love sports of the Absolute—a very lofty ideal. Liberation from the cycle of birth and death, which is the goal of most transcendentalists, is incidental to those engaged in this culture. It is said that the mere reflection of the pure name of Godhead (*namabhasa*), rather than the name proper, terminates the cycle of birth and death. The practical idea of liberation in which one is progressively freed from all of the painful constituents of our life of bondage, such as lust, anger, greed, envy, and pride, is passed over in the course of approaching only the blossoming of the culture of the holy name. Its flower—*prema*, or love of Godhead—belittles liberation as but the other side of the coin of material exploitation. Enjoyment and renunciation, which produce the effects of karma and liberation respectively, are both worldly-centered. One mentality is to "enjoy" the world of illusion (good luck!) and the other is to flee from it. Both mentalities fall short of a transcendental synthesis of these two principles that govern the *mayic* world. Transcendence cannot be the polarization of opposites; it must be a synergy of both. Thus the focus of the servants of the divine name is dedication, through which exploitation and renunciation are harmonized.

If God is light, as the school of renunciation likes to say, then God is surely sound as well, the two being but the same wave vibrating at different frequencies. But God is more than light and sound as we know them. If there is transcendental light, why not sound? Through the medium of sound the world comes into being, and through divine sound it can be properly understood. The *Vedas* and *Upanishads* are called *shruti*, that which is heard. *Upanishad* in particular means to come closer for hearing something confidential. A rather confidential thing to know about the Absolute is his and her name. At least that is a good start.

HALLOWED BE THY NAME

To know the name of the object of our search is the beginning of our finding that truth in a systematic fashion. But it is more than that, because the name of God wholly corresponds with God's personhood.

In the material world of duality, the names of objects, often given so arbitrarily, do not wholly correspond with the object they seek to describe. The *actual* sound of an object brings a profound sense of the object itself. This is so partially even within the world of duality; how much more so is this the case in a realm where sound and object wholly correspond with one another. The name of God and the sound of God, "OM," carry with them the experience of Godhead. And the name more fully than God's sound, for it includes something about the personality of the divine.

The supramental name of God can be heard and sung only when our dedicating nature is directed toward the divine. The name of God will not be possible to understand unless we change the direction of our dedication. We must consider dedication for its own sake if we are to know our highest prospect.

Love, pure love, must be the goal of all existence, and the holy name of God is a "love note" of the divine symphony. It should be allowed to enter our hearts. Actually, if the holy name should desire to descend within our hearts, we cannot check its transcendental current.

ECSTASY—CAN WE LIVE WITHOUT IT?

ECSTASY IS OFTEN USED to refer to the state of rapture experienced at the climax of sense indulgence—sexual union. It is also used in reference to divine states of transcendental love. Do the two have anything in common? Although they are worlds apart, according to some spiritual disciplines, the former is a inverted reflection of the latter. Thus they are similar but not the same.

When we look into a lake at the reflection of a large tree, it appears that the roots are extending upwards and the branches reaching down. Similarly, in this world sexual "ecstasy" appears to be most desirable, while love of Godhead is not a high priority. For most, love of God is no more than a cliché at best: *"Of course I love God."* But the discussion stops there, while sense indulgence continues unchecked, conveniently placing the God one "loves" in the background. Either there's not much at all to say about love of God or long dry philosophical discussions ensue, wherein "God" evaporates into a vague concept that is no different than our own "true self." This vague concept of God is characteristic of all varieties of monism, a philosophy that is presently enjoying an unprecedented following in a world that pines for "oneness."

Genuine monists deny sense indulgence and material emotion, identifying them as products of illusion. This rings rational, and thus monism is often thought of as an improvement over the sensual life and the love of God that sensual addicts keep in the back room. It may be better than the so-called love of mundane sensation-seeking and emotional flutters of sweet nothings. Yet this is so only in a relative sense, for monism, while speaking of God, does away with him altogether. This is so because there is no meaning to God without God's devotees, just as there is no meaning to the devoted without God, whom we devote ourselves to. In the unqualified oneness of no "other," as per the monistic philosophy of the great Shankara, where is there any place for love? For the monistic philosopher, love is an abstract thing—"universal love" or "cosmic love," existence making love with itself at best. This is an underdeveloped state of spiritual love. Oneness must therefore be qualified for it to stand as a philosophy that offers love of God and spiritual ecstasy. Thus neither unqualified monism (*advaita-vedanta*) nor wishful thinking about love of God on the part of sense enjoyers leave much room for higher spiritual love or intimate reciprocal dealings between ourselves and Godhead.

Vaishnava *Vedanta*, which qualifies monism, offers the spiritual seeker greater prospect for love and spiritual ecstasy. Just as our world today earnestly seeks unity yet simultaneously insists on recognizing and honoring cultural differences, so the soul seeks unity with Godhead yet difference from him as well. The beauty of this is that the unity with Godhead sought in Vaishnavism is not compromised by difference, for the difference or eternal individuality of the soul is but a necessary element of transcendental loving exchange. Love of Godhead, that is, requires both God and the devotee of Godhead, each united in love—one in purpose, different in potency. Here oneness lifts us above the duality of material existence, which arises like a great hoax out of the top hat of erroneous sense perception, and difference makes for a spiritual life in which there is the spice of variety.

This ideal is best presented in the Gaudiya Vaishnava school of Sri Chaitanya. Sri Chaitanya exhibited extraordi-

ECSTASY—CAN WE LIVE WITHOUT IT?

nary states of ecstatic rapture never before witnessed in the world, and his followers authored a tightly-reasoned philosophy of divine love, thoroughly referenced from the Vedic scriptures. In this school we find concrete love, as opposed the abstract love of monism. It is divine love replete with reciprocal dealings, devoid of the sense of separateness we suffer from in this world of dualities. Sri Chaitanya posits oneness or union in love (*rasam anandam*) above mere identification with the substance of the spiritual plane *(Brahman)*, which is the shortsighted goal of the monist. Inconceivable as it may seem, as audacious as it may sound, Sri Chaitanya proclaims that we can actually love God as we do our friend, our child, or our lover. For Sri Chaitanya, love of Godhead is a priority of such magnitude that meeting this necessity fulfills all other needs. In his ideology, all forms of love find their fulfillment in Godhead alone. Their reflected forms, in which Godhead is not central, are illusory. For Sri Chaitanya, lust and love (*kama* and *prema*) have much in common, although they are at the same time very different. *Kama* is only the reflection of *prema*.

The annals of the devotional school of Sri Chaitanya delineate a veritable science of ecstatic love. Mundane love pales in comparison to this ecstatic love, and abstract love—the bliss of *Brahman*—serves only as a foundation for this love's further development. Ecstasy for the *bhaktas* (devotees) consists of dozens of internal states of divine rapture, all of which have corresponding psychological and physiological manifestations. These symptoms are observable, and for those who know the devotional science of love of God, they indicate the extent of one's internal development. Thus in the study of divine ecstasy we find just what our rational twentieth century mindset insists upon: verifiable evidence.

ANCIENT WISDOM

But wait—although we can observe it, ecstasy eludes the rational mind just the same. What are we observing? And what are our instruments of observation? We are observing only the psychological and physiological expressions of something that we have no direct access to with the limited instruments of sense perception and rational thought. The symptoms of ecstatic love observed in the bodies of saints can only be identified as such after having received knowledge of how to identify ecstatic symptoms from those in whom they manifest. Otherwise our minds, like vultures, seek to adulterate the descent of spiritual truths, turning the living into the dead. And when our rational appetite attempts to devour divine love, we taste only the bottle and not the nectar inside. The result is a bad case of spiritual indigestion.

If we can begin with the premise that divine states—not merely extended physical or mental states—exist, we are halfway home. The second half of the journey toward understanding ecstasy will require hearing from the right source, for there are many impostors. Then, with our faith aroused, we will have to venture into the realm of our own experience of these things. Although this second requirement is rather demanding, can we really be content to live without ecstasy? Existence without cognizance is meaningless. And mere cognizance of the nature of our existence lacks the ecstasy for which our hearts and souls yearn. In a sense we are already in search of ecstasy—we are pleasure seekers, *raso vai sah*. A thorough study of the *Upanishads*, which on the surface advise us to understand that which we are not (*neiti, neiti*, not this, not this), reveals a deeper message: *srinvantu visve amritasya putrah*, we are descendants of ecstasy, we belong to a land of nectar. We exist for joy's sake, but we are now living in sorrow. Ecstasy is our birthright, yet the devotional school tells us that

ECSTASY—CAN WE LIVE WITHOUT IT?

we are looking for it in the wrong place, in the reflection rather than in the image of reality itself.

In search of ecstasy we can look to some of the devotional literature in which ecstasy is expounded on. The *Bhakti Rasamrita Sindhu* of the sixteenth century devotional mystic and principal disciple of Sri Chaitanya, Srila Rupa Goswami, serves as an excellent guide. This extraordinary book is but one of many such books compiled at about the same time by various authors, all of whom were members of Sri Chaitanya's cult of transcendental love. Rupa Goswami is accepted as the leading exponent on the subject of divine ecstasy. He has been dubbed *rasacharya*, or one who is expert in relishing the humors of transcendental ecstasy.

To describe Sri Chaitanya's conception of divine love in terms we might understand, Rupa Goswami borrowed from the theory of *rasa* (mellows of loving exchange) found in orthodox Sanskrit poetry. Making necessary modifications, he constructed a framework, employing this secular concept in order to explain the selfless transcendental love mentioned in the *Bhagavat Purana*. In so doing, he and his followers have been careful to distinguish, for example, Krishna's spiritual love relationship with the milkmaids (*gopis*) of Vraja—which has been so much misunderstood by scholars and abused as a license for sensual indulgence in the name of spiritual pursuit—from the affairs of ordinary men and women.

Krishna's love affairs, although bearing the outward resemblance of the "love" of illusioned souls for one another, is categorically different according to Rupa Goswami. The latter, which mundane poets praise, is really based on the demands that our material senses impose on us. Responding to these sensual demands creates off-center relationships. Thus they do not endure and cannot fulfill the soul. But a relationship with the transcendental Deity is one that is properly centered. God *is* the center, and to perceive otherwise is illusion. Only when we understand this point and relate with one another accordingly can our relationships with one another be considered spiritual.

The *Bhakti-rasamrita-sindhu* mentions eight basic symptoms of transcendental emotions, *sattvika bhavas*. These conditions of spiritual emotion appear when the devotee develops *priti,* or pure love of Godhead. They are the happiness that is derived as a byproduct of offering oneself in love. This happiness is categorically different from the "happiness" of one steeped in a separate sense of self; that is, the self as having a separate purpose from the purpose of the Godhead. Transcendental happiness endures both in separation and union, for it is derived from the happiness of Godhead and not ourselves. The beloved's (Godhead's) happiness creates the happiness of the devotee offering his or her love; thus, the devotee's happiness is not something that is consciously pursued, yet it is nonetheless a symptom of attainment of the goal.

Although there are obvious similarities between ecstasy and psychic states of experience, such as the arousal of the *kundalini shakti,* the two are different. Ecstasy is derived from above, and no amount of effort exerted from below can bring it about. This is fundamental to a pure theistic ideology. That is, we cannot produce the experience of love of Godhead any more than we can produce God. "Matter Motherism," although a popular theory, is no more than that—popular, but not practical. Pure theism rightfully asserts that any material manifestation is but an idea. It is a conscious concept. Matter is within consciousness; it is not that consciousness is within matter, only to "take birth" after a protracted pregnancy and later "give birth" to the Supreme consciousness. Grace is required for communion with divinity. And chemical (there is even a new drug called ecstasy), physical, and mental maneuvers that adjust our ner-

ECSTASY—CAN WE LIVE WITHOUT IT?

vous system to produce exhilarating, "blissful" effects are not the same as the experience of ecstatic love of Godhead.

The symptoms of ecstatic love are manifested physiologically via the nervous system resulting from psychological states generated from the development of *prema*. In this condition, some parts of our nervous system that ordinarily do not function are brought to life. Kundalini arousal may also be affected, but here the cause of this physiological phenomenon is spiritual (the arousal of the kundalini may also be stimulated by material means). These spiritual expressions do not disturb the inner serenity of the soul, whose life blossoms as they manifest. Only the equilibrium of the mind and body, being unaccustomed to the high pressure created in the mind of one anointed with transcendental emotion, appear disturbed.

The eight ecstatic transformations are: *stamba* (becoming stunned), *sveda* (perspiration), *romancha* (hairs standing on end), *sarva-bhanga* (inability to speak), *kampa* (trembling), *vaivarnya* (change of bodily color), *ashru* (tears), and *pralaya* (loss of external consciousness). These are accompanied by thirteen *anubhavas*, or subsequent transcendental emotions. Rupa Goswami explains that the eight ecstatic transformations are expressed outwardly as the soul absorbed in ecstatic love comes into contact with the five elemental constituents of the material experience (the subtle principles of solidity, liquidity, heat, movement, and space, represented for convenience as earth, water, fire, air, and sky). When in touch with earth (solidity), one appears stunned, like stone. When in touch with water (liquidity), there is shedding of tears. When in connection with fire (heat), there is perspiration. When in touch with air (movement), there is trembling, faltering of the voice, and standing of the bodily hairs on end. Contact with sky (space) produces loss of external consciousness and change of bodily color.

ANCIENT WISDOM

In some instances, such as the ecstatic manifestations of Sri Chaitanya at Jagannatha Puri, these transformations are known to assume extreme proportions. The shedding of tears if aroused as a result of transcendental jubilation are very cold. If they arise out of spiritual anger, they become hot. But in either case the eyes become reddish or sometimes white and swollen, pouring tears as if from a syringe. For Sri Chaitanya, trembling of the body involved his joints elongating and his body stretching. At one point the limbs of his body withdrew inside his body's trunk, like a tortoise, while his teeth chattered such that they appeared to come loose from his jaws and come out of his mouth. All of these descriptions certainly seem shocking, undesirable, and a far cry from what we would ordinarily think of as ecstasy. But we cannot judge by the surface. After all, our present mental and physical conditions, normal as we think of them, are not affording us the ecstasy our souls crave.

Except in extreme cases, the devotees are able to check these symptoms from being expressed through the nervous system, although they continue to rage within. This is an accepted practice among genuine saints who seek to avoid drawing attention to themselves. Their transcendental love affair is kept as private as we would keep our own on the material plane; it is not something to talk about all over town. But when the purest devotees are overpowered by spiritual excitement, they cannot check themselves. Just as when the moon rises and the ordinarily grave and sober ocean becomes agitated, so the ordinarily grave devotees have been known to give way to spiritual emotion, and thus these symptoms surface in rare circumstances.

Although keeping these symptoms in check, the genuine devotees often keep themselves in the public eye, advocating their cause of devotion. In so doing they expose those who learn to manipulate their nervous systems such

ECSTASY—CAN WE LIVE WITHOUT IT?

that mild forms of some of these symptoms appear in their bodies. The cause of such developments is not spiritual emotion. Just as there are different causes for and motives behind the same physical expression in different persons, so there may be different causes for the release of psychic energy resulting in similar bodily transformations. For example, ordinary tears (a particular biological manifestation) may be derived either from sadness or joy, opposites. The imitative symptoms of ecstasy are a product of the world of sadness, while genuine ecstatic symptoms are derived from the plane of joy (*anandam*).

Those who are experts in transcendental loving affairs are able to detect the specific spiritual position of another by external symptoms. That is, they can determine who the Deity of another is and to what degree a transcendental relationship has developed with that Deity. Despite endeavors to check ecstatic symptoms, traces of them are still perceivable by those who themselves experience such ecstatic symptoms. In effect, an unspoken language exists between experiencers. As one may know the country from which another hails by the manner of his or her dress or speech, the experiencers understand one another's positions by their symptoms.

For those of us who are not experiencers, Rupa Goswami advises that we not look directly for the ecstatic symptoms, but for the dawning of inner awakening in the form of the preliminary symptoms of love of Godhead. This stage is technically called *rati*. The emotion known as *rati* is transpsychological. It is the first ray of the dawning sun of transcendental love on the spiritual horizon, which penetrates deeply within the heart of the *bhakta*. The observable circumstances that surround its development are ninefold: serenity of the mind in the face of circumstances that warrant disturbance (*ksanti*), extreme care not to allow a moment

ANCIENT WISDOM

to pass outside of the service of Godhead *(avyartha-kalata)*, distaste for objects of the senses *(virakti)*, pridelessness *(manasunyata)*, firm faith that the goal of love will be achieved by God's grace *(asabandha)*, intense eagerness to attain the goal *(samutkantha)*, attraction for the transcendental name of God *(nama gane sada rucih)*, natural inclination to discuss the transcendental qualities of Godhead *(tad gunakhyane asaktih)*, and a strong desire to live in a holy place of pilgrimage where one of the incarnations of God has descended *(tad vasati sthale pritih)*. Those who conduct themselves in this way are worthy of our respect.

The devotional tradition of Sri Chaitanya further holds that the transcendental realm is not formless. The concept of the transcendental form and personhood of Godhead is an essential element in the ontology of ecstasy. Without it there is no question of emotion, reciprocal dealings, or the subsequent realm in which all such spiritual activity takes place. To insist that the truth *must* be formless is only a negative reaction to the obvious shortcomings of material form, which is the cause of material separateness and disharmony. The transcendental realm inhabited by transcendental personalities with spiritual forms is transtemporal—in it eternality and the passage of time are harmonized; unity and difference exist simultaneously in a higher synthesis. There, the motivation for all action is love—love of Godhead replete with all of the emotions we experience in materially embodied life, only of spiritual character.

Imagine the healthy expression of each and every one of our human emotions. Currently we struggle with our emotions. They deviate us from reason, and spiritual life is at least reasonable. Drowning in an ocean of emotions, we may consider that eradicating all emotional expression through rational thought will ensure the brightest

ECSTASY—CAN WE LIVE WITHOUT IT?

future. But that is a life without ecstasy. Relief from our present condition, yes. But ecstasy, no.

The devotional transcendentalists suggest that the entire picture of material existence must be turned around. Everything has its healthy expression. This means that our typically Western concept of God on his throne keeping score from the clouds, blessing and condemning, is at best a lesser theistic conception. That God cannot be loved in the way we express our love for our friend, our child, or our lover. For example, the various emotions of fraternal love, which bring intimacy allowing us to relax with or even lovingly oppose our friend, are not the kind of loving dealings we ordinarily think of exchanging with God. But according to Sri Chaitanya, all loving propensities originate in the transcendental realm, and they are only reflected in the material plane of perception. Thus, rather than seeing God as one's father, one can even develop the spiritual emotions *of a father,* loving Godhead paternally, or in the optimum, one may develop amorous love for Godhead!

Many people have summarily rejected the fatherly God—"Our Father who art in Heaven"—who has for so long dominated Western theology. Today, the dynamics of this concept, or lack of the same, insults the intelligence of most progressive people who are seeking unity and freedom from the duality of a subject/object world. But perhaps we are lacking only the proper explanation of this ultimate phenomenon of the personhood of Godhead and lacking an explanation of the potential for higher, more intimate loving relationships with the divine as well. Such explanations have been postulated by Rupa Goswami, and there are volumes of literature to explore in this connection. The modern-day follower of Rupa Goswami and Sri Chaitanya, Swami B. R. Sridhara, my own eternal preceptor, has called this the "Krishna conception of Godhead."

ANCIENT WISDOM

Krishna is not an old man, but an eternal youth. He dances and frolics with the milkmaids of Vrindavana in a form (*vigraha*) that is *sac-cid-ananda,* full of eternality, knowledge, and ecstasy. Once the dynamics of this concept are resolved in one's mind, and it is clear that unity in love with Godhead outshines mere unity in principle, the prospect of a life of ecstasy dawns.

Thus, according to Rupa Goswami, ecstasy as we know it in embodied life has some connection with the divine sense of the term: it is its inverted reflection. The logic is simple: nothing in a reflection can exist without being present in the original image, but a reflection can never substitute for the real thing. For those interested in spiritual life, no amount of caution here is too much. Lust is not love. The real image is not to be interpreted in terms of its reflection, rather the reflection is to be interpreted in terms of the original image. As long as we are unable to rise above the shadowy world of the senses, transcendental love will elude us. It is sensible to aspire for a life beyond the dualities created by sense perception. But until that time when we have learned to walk spiritually, access to transcendental love lies in hearing from those saints and sages who have attained the ultrasensory realm.

From the reflection one can come to know something about the real image. In the reflection of love we actively seek out our enjoyment, exploiting others for our sensual ends. The end result is a drama of suffering with a curtain call of death and a demand for a repeat performance. In the love world of Sri Chaitanya, one actively seeks only service. The curtain never closes, and even any apparent suffering is full of transcendental joy.

ABOUT THE AUTHOR

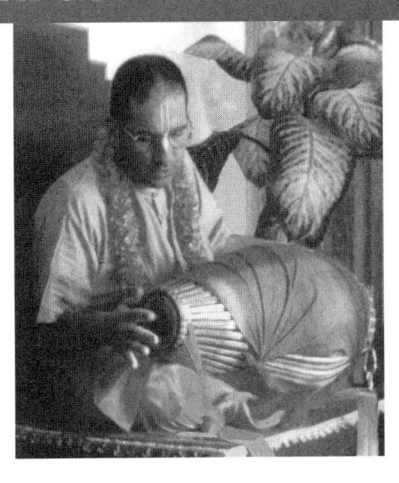

SWAMI B.V. TRIPURARI
was initiated into the Gaudiya Vaishnava *sampradaya* by A. C. Bhaktivedanta Swami Prabhupāda in 1972. In 1975 in Vrindavana, India, he accepted the renounced order of life from Bhaktivedanta Swami and has since become one of his most influential disciples.

In 1985 Swami Tripurari founded the Gaudiya Vaishnava Society, now an international movement with *ashramas* in the United States, Europe, and India. Since 1988, Swami Tripurari has served as senior editor and publisher of the *Clarion Call*, an international periodical promoting experiential spirituality. He is the author of numerous articles on the Gaudiya Vaishnava philosophy and culture. His first book, *Rasa: Love Relationships in Transcendence*, is now in its second printing.

At present, Swami Tripurari travels extensively and can be reached at Sri Sri Gaura-Nityananda Audarya Ashrama, 325 River Road, Eugene, OR 97404.

REFERENCES

Anthony, Ecker, and Wilber, *Spiritual Choices* (New York: Paragon House Publishers, 1987).

Being Beautiful, reprinted from FDA consumer report, November 1986 by Dori Stehlin.

Berendt, Joachim-Ernst, *Nada Brahma: The World Is Sound* (Rochester, Vermont: Inner Traditions, 1987).

Bhaktivedanta Swami, *Nectar of Devotion* (Los Angeles: Bhaktivedanta Book Trust, 1972).

Business Week Feb. 8th, 1988.

Freedland, Nat, *The Occult Explosion* (East Rutherford, New Jersey: G.P. Putnam's Sons, 1927).

Geldern, Dr. Robert Heine, "Challenge to Isolationists," *Hindu America* (New Delhi: Zodiac Press, 1940).

Ingram, Catherine, *Following in the Footsteps of Ghandi* (Berkeley, California: Parallax Press, 1990).

McClain, Earnest G., *The Myth of Invariance* (New York: Nicolas Hays Inc., 1976).

McClellen, Randall, *The Healing Forces of Music* (Boston: Amity House, 1988).

Mirsea, Eliade, *Yoga: Immortality and Freedom* (New York: Bollinfen Foundation Inc., 1958).

Mishlove, Jeff, *Life After Life* (New York: Bantam Books, 1981).

Mishra Rammurti S., *The Textbook of Yoga Psychology* (New York: Julian Press, 1963).

Mitra, Kana, "Theologizing Through History?" *Toward a Universal Theology of Religion* (Maryknoll, New York: Orbis Books, 1987).

ANCIENT WISDOM

Smith, Wilfred Cantwell, "Theology of the World's Religious History," *Toward a Universal Theology of Religion* (Maryknoll, New York: Orbis Books, 1987).

Swami B. R. Sridhara, *Loving Search for the Lost Servant* (San Jose, California: Guardian of Devotion Press, 1987).

Swami Hariharayananda Aranya, *Yoga Philosophy of Patanjali* (Albany, New York: Suny Press, 1983).

Tame, David, *The Secret Power of Music* (Rochester, Vermont: Inner Traditions, 1984).

INDEX

A
abortion 70
abstinence. *See* continence
achintya bhedabheda 21
Adolph, Jonathon 127
AIDS 70
allergic reactions from fragrances 86
allopathy
  discontentment with 102
  disease causation, cure 100–102
  investigated ayurveda 102–103
altruism 111
anima 123
animal experimentation 88
Ankor 33
Anthony, Dick 109
anubhavas 153
anuman 95
Aristotle 129
aromatherapists 90, 91
aromatics 88
  used in Jewish tradition 87
Aryans 32
  conquests 32–35
asana 120
Asians, discovered America 28, 29
ashru 153
ashta siddhis. See *maha siddhis*
atoms 139
attachment, subtle material 132
ayurveda 87, 93
  conceptual framework 95–99
  disease causation, cure 100–101
  investigated by allopathy 102–103
  methodology 94–95
  origin 98–99
  surgery 95
Aztec culture 34–35

B
babies 77. *See also* fetus
Babylon 31
Basham, A. L. ix
Bering Strait, crossing the 30
Bhagavad-gita 18-19
  on channeling 130
Bhagavat Purana 17–18, 80
Bhakti Rasamrita Sindhu 151
Bible
  on channeling 130
bindi 87
birth, traumatic
  effects on psychic abilities 80
Bock, Dick 59
Bolden, Buddy 51
botanical medicine 89
brahma-tejas 74
brahmacharya 74
Brahman 143
Brott, Boris 79
Brown-Sequard 73–74
Buddha 113
Buddhism 14, 24

deep ecology movement 15
bullocks 41

C

Cambodia (Kamboja) 33
Cantwell, Wilfred Smith 27
Capra, Fritjof 15
Cartesian dualism 20
caste system. See *varnashrama*
cause and effect 122
Cayce, Edgar 54, 132
Chaitanya Charitamrta 23
Chaitanya, Sri 108, 113, 148–149. See also *acintya bhedabheda;* Vaishnava Vedanta
  ecstatic manifestations 154
  ideology of 149
channeling 128
  denounced by every major religious tradition 130
  not divine 133
  reasons for popularity 129
  vs. inspired side of saints 130
Charaka Samhita 100
Charkrovosky, Igor 80
Charlton, Henry Bastian 30
Chia, Mantak 72
Christ 113, 135
  mentioned in *Bavishya Purana* 37
civilizations, comparison of 33
Coltrane, John 52, 59, 60
Columbus 27, 29
compassion
  human vs. spiritual 113
  imitation 110

material 114
spiritual 113
synthesis of happiness and distress 107
Congress of the Americanists 31
consciousness, compared to ocean 143
continence 65
  benefits of
    health 71–74
    spiritual 74–75
  civilizations that practiced 67
  education 70
  solves major social dilemmas 70
cosmetics 85
  birth defects 85
  carcinogenic 85
cows, *zebu.* See also sacred cow, India's
  dung 45–46
  effects of modernization on 42
  essential to India's economy 45
  sick and aged cows 44

D

Dass, Ram 114
Davis, Andrew Jackson 129
Davis, Miles 51
Deadwyler, William 11
DeBroglie 139
dedication
  qualifier of consciousness 139
  to holy name 140

INDEX

deep ecology movement 14–17, 20, 24
   Buddhism 15
descending knowledge 103
dharana 120
dhyana 120
diffusionist theory 29
disease causation, cure 100–102
doshadhatus 96
drugs, synthetic 88

E

Eastern spirituality
   environmental crisis 14
Ecker, Bruce 109
ecstasy 147
   eludes rational mind 150
   for *bhaktas* 149
   reflection of 158
   symptoms 150
   symptoms can be checked 154
   symptoms imitated 154–155
   symptoms of 153
   vs. psychic states 152
Egypt 31
Ekholm, Gordon 33
electromagnetic forces 121
elementargedanke. *See* physico-chemical evolution
Ellis, Don 55
Emancipation Proclamation 129
emotions 156
enlightened thinking 135
enlightenment 112
environmental crisis

Christianity 13
   deep ecology 14–17
   Eastern spirituality 14
epidemic of arms 100–101
era of reason, European 99
essential oils 86, 90–91
   used by ancient civilizations 87
   used by Aztecs 87
   used by Hindus 87
   used to treat war victims 89
Europe 35
   Industrial Revolution 37
   Inquisition, the 36
   Palace of Versailles 36
   printing press 36
Experience of No Self, The 134

F

farming 41
FDA 85
Ferguson, Marilyn 127
fetus
   experience in womb 79, 81
   flash of pure consciousness 83–84
   personality development of 79–80
   spiritual development of 79–80
feudal system. *See varnashrama*
fragrances 85
   affect psychic and mental states 90
   allergic reactions 86
French Revolution 10
Freud 79

G

Gaia hypothesis 16
Gandhi 71
Gattefosse, Rene Maurice 89
gaurava 100
Gleason, Ralph 59
God
  not formless 156
  Western concept of 157
  Western concept of
    rejected 157
God, name of. *See* holy name
Grasse, France 88
greed *(adana)* 100
Greens, the 14
Guthrie, K. S. 73

H

hair dye 86
Halpern, Stephen 60
Haraldsson, Erlendur 117
Hare Krishna *mantra* 60
Harrison, George 60
hearing, importance of
  137–139
hoarding *(sanchaya)* 100
holy name 137, 145
  as God incarnate 140
  as means and ends 143
  dedication to brings
    fulfillment 140
  not mundane 141
  perfection of the culture of
    143
  primary (direct) names
    142
  secondary names 141
  supramental 143
  to achieve liberation 142

Horn, Paul 59
human potential movement
  127
humanism 133
Humbolt, Alexander von 29
humility 23
hunger 115
Huxley, Aldous 125

I

incense 87
India 39–40, 57. *See also*
  ayurveda; cows, *zebu;*
  raga; sacred cow, India's
  as source of civilization 32
  as source of earthly spiritu-
    ality 37
  farming 41
  foreign domination 93
  history 28–29
  modernization 46–47
  Western influence on 40
insensitivity 109
intellectual class. *See*
  varnashrama
intelligence 131
  in the mode of goodness 82
  in the mode of ignorance
    83
  in the mode of passion
    82–83
invisibility 123
ishita 124
isolationist theory 29

J

Java 33
jazz
  influenced by *raga* 51–52

INDEX

origins 50–51
spiritual aspects 58

K

kamavasayita 124
kampa 153
kapha 96
kardil 86–87
karma 101
karmic disposition 7
Kaviraja Goswami 23
Kayser, Hans 138
knowledge, acquiring
   Western approach 94
knowledge of past, present,
   and future 122
Krishna 158
   love affairs of 151
kundalini 153

L

laboring class. *See*
   varnashrama
laghima 123
Lal, Chaman 33
Lappe, Frances Moore 42
Lazarus 133
laziness *(alasya)* 100
lethargy *(shrama)* 100
levitation 121–122
levitation, psychic 122
life, beginning of
   opinion of mystics 78–79
   opinion of popular religion 77
   opinion of scientists 77
limbic system 90
Lincoln, Abraham 129
listening, importance of 139

lobha 100
Lovelock, James 16

M

MacLaine, Shirley 128
Macumba 128
maha siddhis 123–125
   accomplished by modern
   science 124–125
Mahabharata 18
mahima (garima) 123
martial class. *See varnashrama*
Maslow, Abraham 127
matter motherism 152
Maury, Marguerite 89
maya 107
Mayan civilization 34
medicine, modern. *See*
   allopathy
Mehta, Gita x
Mena, Ramon 34
mental realm 132
mercantile class. *See*
   varnashrama
mind 131
mind reading 123
Mitra, Kana 28
monism
   denies sense indulgence 147
   does away with God 148
   no place for love 148
monists 142
mridanga (khol) 52
music. *See also raga*
   as medicine 54
   Western 50
mystic perfections, eight. *See*
   maha siddhis
mystic power 117, 118

N

Naess, Arne 14
namabhasa 144
neo-Aristotelian paradigm 99
new age
  as a religion 128
  as diverse group 127
  industries 128
  influenced by human potential movement 127
  roots in jazz 60
Nixon, Richard 133
niyama 120

O

ojas 75
"old spiritual age" 128, 129–130, 134
olfactory nerves 90
OM 145
Orwell, George 125
overpopulation 70

P

Palenque, Chiapas, tribes of 34
parapsychology 119
parigraha 100
pasteurization 46
Patanjali Muni 118, 124
perfumery 88
philanthropy 111–112
philosophers 132
physicochemical evolution (*elementargedanke*) 30
pitta 96
Plato 129
Plutarch 134
Poindexter, Ambassador 34
positive mental attitude (PMA) 133
Prahlad 113
prakamya 124
prakriti nirvana 24
pralaya 153
pramana 94
pranayama 120
prapti siddhi 124
pratyahara 120
pratyaksha 95
pregaphone 79
prema 144
prenatal psychology 79
Protestant Reformation 10
psychic abilities
  effect of traumatic birth on 80
psychological analysis 122
psychology, modern 119
psychosexual theories, Western 71
Puranas 28
Pythagoras 72

R

raga 50, 52, 55–56
  composition 56
  conception of time 56
  miracles 54
  training 52
rajas 97
rasa, theory of 151
rasadhatu 96
rati, development of 155
reductionist worldview 101
reincarnation
  Westernized 133
Renaissance 17

INDEX

renunciation 110–111
  false 109–110
Rifkin, Jeremy x
Roberts, Bernadette 134
Rogers, Carl 127
romancha 153
Rupa Goswami, Srila 151
Russian Revolution 10

S

shabda pramana 95
sacred cow, India's 39. *See also* cows, *zebu*
  criticism of 43–44
  how farmers view their cows 44
  religious beliefs 42–43
Sai Baba 117
saints 135
samadhi 120
samyama 120, 120–121
sannyasa 75
saptadhatu 96
sarva-bhanga 153
sattva 97
sattvika bhavas 152
Schlesinger, Albert 3
science, modern xi–xii
scientific approach, modern
  problems with 97
  process of acquiring knowledge 94
sex desire
  affected by diet 68–69
sexual "ecstasy" 147
sexual energy 65–67
  uses of 71
Shank, Bud 59
Shankar, Ravi 52–53, 59

Shankara, Adi 113
Shushruta Samhita 95
siddhis. See *maha siddhis;* mystic power
Sidenbladh, Erik 80
smell, sense of 90
Socrates 129
sound
  importance of 137, 139
  inventions 140
  the world as 139
Sovatsky, Stuart 75
Spiritual Choices 109
spiritual life 112
  genuine 113, 135
  pitfalls of 109–112
  pseudo 112
Sridhara, Swami B. R. 157
stamba 153
suffering 114–115
suicide 132
Shukadeva Goswami 83
sveda 153

T

tamas 97
temezcalls 87
tilak 87
Time magazine 128
Tirro, Frank 51
Tisserand, Robert B. 91
trance channelers 128
transcendence 144
transcendent experience 107
transpersonal psychology 119
tridosha 96
triguna 97
truth, axiomatic 134

U

unctuarium 88
UNESCO 102
UNIDO 102
unity of nature 23
Upanishads 150

V

Vaishnava *Vedanta* 148
  environmental crisis 16–25
vaivarnya 153
varnashrama
  ashrama 8
  compared to a body 6
  compared to feudal system 9–11
  spiritual equality 6
  varna 6–7
  vitiated forms of
    capitalism 5, 10–12
    communism 5, 10–12
    modern India 5
vashita 124
vata 96
Vedanta 107
Vedas
  view of mental world 131
vegetarianism 68, 69
Verny, Thomas 79
Vietnam (Champa) 33
Virel, Andre 90
voodoo 51

W

Wald, George 78
White, Lynn, Jr. 13
WHO 102
Wilber, Ken 109

Y

yama 120
yoga 119
Yoga Sutras 118, 121
Yudhisthira Maharaja 18

Z

zebu. *See* cows, *zebu*